Seven Deadly Sins of Dying Churches

iUniverse books may be ordered through booksellers or by contacting:

iUniverse
1663 Liberty Drive
Bloomington, IN 47403
www.iuniverse.com
1-800-Authors (1-800-288-4677)

Because of the dynamic nature of the Internet, any Web addresses or links contained in this book may have changed since publication and may no longer be valid.

ISBN: 978-1-4401-4628-2 (sc)
ISBN: 978-1-4401-4629-9 (ebk)

Printed in the United States of America

iUniverse rev. date: 8/20/2009

SEVEN DEADLY SINS OF DYING CHURCHES

WILLIAM G. JUSTICE
DMIN, DPHIL, DLITT.

IUNIVERSE, INC.
NEW YORK   BLOOMINGTON

Dedicated to

The Rev. Dr. Hollis Green,

visionary, scholar, author, founder

of

Oxford Graduate School,

and

Oasis University, Trinidad

mentor, and friend

for more than thirty years

Other Books By William G. Justice

Guilt and Forgiveness
(How God Can Help You Feel Good About Yourself)

Don't Sit on the Bed
(A Handbook for Visiting the Sick)

Guilt, the Source and the Solution
(Defense Systems to Avoid Feeling Guilty)

When Death Comes
(A Handbook for Pastors and Laypersons Who Minister to the Bereaved)

When Your Patient Dies
(A Handbook for Physicians and Nurses
Who Minister to Families at the Time of a Patient's Death)

Jesus' Silent Years: Facts the Gospels Do Not Tell Us

More Than A Social Call
(a Guidebook for Visiting the Sick)

God in the Hands of Angry Sinners

Jesus the Maverick King

The Nature of God as Revealed in Jesus

Training Guide for Visiting the Sick: More than a Social Call

When God Seems Silent

Damned if We Are Not Forgiven; Understanding Guilt and People Who Are Their Own Worst Enemies

What if Jesus Remained in the Tomb? World Changes Brought About by Christianity

Gifts for the Gods: Pagan and Christian Sacrifices

CONTENTS

Contents

INTRODUCTION

For many years, the secular world often has looked at the church of North America with disgust. "It's dead," some have said. "It's irrelevant," said others. "It's a club of the self-righteous," said still more. "It makes no real improvement in the world, or even in individual lives," others charge. Most simply ignore it. We of the church have rarely paused long enough to examine the accusations for some element of truth.

When words of criticism have reached the muffled ears of the modern church, we have self-righteously failed to show enough respect for the critics to give them any credibility. Like a fat giant, the church has barely roused from its slumber, grunted, "Not so," rolled over and sunk back into a state of unconsciousness. If the church has stirred at all, it has rubbed its sleepy eyes and pointed to some of its true saints and many faithful ministers without looking at the larger body of those who profess its faith. If you think I exaggerate, be patient.

When I speak of the *modern* church, my use of the word "modern" has no direct reference to the "modern" and "post-modern" schools of philosophical thought. When I speak of the sin of the "modern" church, I speak of the church of today—the church at large of the early twenty-first century.

I've long held a fascination with the message of Jesus. For the harlot, the traitorous tax collectors, and "sinners," He showed compassion, tenderness, and patience. But for the Pharisees and Sadducees— the leaders of the organized religion of His beloved Jewish people, Jesus made blistering attacks. He called them snakes, and whitewashed tombs. When He pointed to their sin, they pointed to their tithes and their sacrifices. We can only wonder what He wants to say to those of us who make up the modern church.

If someone points out a weakness in the church, we are tempted to point to some strength, without looking for possible truth in the critical statement. In the marriage counseling office, if a woman points to the fact that her husband never takes her out for fun time together, he angrily points out her error. "You forget! I recently took you out to dinner and a movie. You even talked about how much you enjoyed it." She responds, "Yes, we did. That was more than two years ago." First century Jews did not want to hear of their sin, spouses do not want to hear of their sin, and the church has pointed to its many successes, while refusing to look at the sin within it.

A story has been told that a reporter once said to President Abraham Lincoln, "Mr. President, General Harrison has called you a fool. What is your response to General Harrison?" Mr. Lincoln is said to have slowly scratched his beard and replied, "I respect General Harrison's opinion. I guess I'd better examine his statement and see what truth I can find in it." Perhaps we of the modern church should listen more closely to our critics. It has been said that the only people who tell us the truth about ourselfves are those who despise us most and those who love us the most.

Before we go any further, let me state clearly that I truly love Christ's church. It has been an important part of my life for more than seventy years. I began attending regularly with my parents when I was only age three. By the time I went away to college, I had received awards for not having missed attending Sunday School for more than seven years. I'm a graduate of a denominational university, and earned my Masters degree at a denominational seminary. My two and a half years of Internship and Residency in training for ministry as a hospital chaplain were completed in a hospital owned by a Protestant denomination. Two of my doctoral degrees were earned in institutions with firm Christian foundations. My honorary doctoral degree, awarded as the results of three additional post-doctoral research projects; also was awarded by a Christian graduate school. I've listened in the classrooms. I've taught in the classrooms. I've listened from the pew, and I've preached from the pulpit. I've led music, served communion, taken offerings, and in my retirement years while I write this, I serve as a deacon in my church and serve as a member of a team who ministers to people who are homebound.

You may sense irritation sometimes while you read. Since I am a retired hospital chaplain, I learned many years ago that when people weep, they often speak with a note of anger in their voice. During my earlier years, I could not understand why writers have called Jeremiah the weeping prophet. You need not remind me that I am no Jeremiah, but having struggled with the sins of modern churches, I think I may better understand at least some of Jeremiah's sorrow. And I think I may better understand my Lord's tears when He wept over the city of Jerusalem.

I love the church! It was for her that Christ surrendered Himself to suffer and die on a cross for the sin of humankind. It is the church that is truly the Bride of the resurrected Christ. It is only because I love His church that I must endure the pain of charging a major segment of the modern church with living in sin! The words "major segment" recognizes exceptions. You will be able to point to exceptions to every sweeping statement that I will make. Let us thank God for those exceptions. They are the ones who are helping to keep the church alive. However, churches all across America are unnecessarily dying. After an adequate diagnosis, they can be treated and perhaps their lives can be saved.

Since I am going to have much to say about the definitions of words in the pages ahead, let's begin with some definitions here. Already, I have made repeated references to the "church." Since I have done little traveling outside the continental United States for many years, I can speak only of that which I see in the United States, and perhaps of what I have read that is happening in the United Kingdom.[1] However, that of which I speak is from personal knowledge of what I know of churches in the United States of America. I'll let others make their observations about the church in other countries.

Unfortunately, when people speak of the Church, they often are assumed to refer to the Roman Catholic Church. Although I include the Roman Catholic Church in my concern, throughout this book, when I speak of the church, I refer to *all* organized Christianity in the United States.

I am fully aware that in the New Testament, with few exceptions, the word church relates to a local body of believers. I refer to both, the thousands of local churches and the larger body that makes up Christ's Universal Church.

And when I speak of the "sin" of the modern church, I use the classical Hebrew definition of sin as borrowed from the language of the archer who shoots at a target and "misses the mark." The word "sin" can also mean to err or wander from the path of uprightness, or to violate God's law.

Many years ago, while studying the New Testament, I became aware that everything Jesus asked His followers to do was ultimately for the benefit of His follower and/or the follower's neighbor. Later, I realized that all of the Ten Commandments that God gave the Israelites through Moses on Mt. Sinai were for the benefit of His people. Even later, I realized that because He loves humankind, everything that God has ever asked of his people has always been for the benefit of His people. If all behaviors directed by God is for the benefit of human beings, sin may be understood as any behavior or attitude that harms any human being or fails to promote the best interests of any human being. Such behavior is in violation of the established will of God, an offense against the part of His nature that loves and demands love. In brief, I sin when I do anything that harms any human being—even the one who lives in my skin. Still further, I sin any time I fail to do that which promotes the true welfare of any human being—even the one who lives in my skin.

I truly try to remain gender-sensitive as I write. However, even after more than thirty-five years of writing for publication, his/her, his or her, his-her wording sometimes creates such clumsy sentences for me that I revert to the use of the masculine gender to refer to all members of the human race. Please accept that I am truly gender-respectful and forgive me for that limitation as a writer. I, too, remain a work in progress.

After having read an early draft of this book, a friend commented, "Bill, I don't like your book. It is too negative." Therefore, I decided to place this book "on the back burner" to "simmer." Soon afterward, my darling wife of 54 years, who had been in declining health for roughly 12 years, was diagnosed with cancer. She died seven weeks and two days after the diagnosis. Almost two years later, I married one of the most loving women left on our planet. Only two months into our marriage, doctors diagnosed her cancer. She died seven weeks and six days after the diagnosis. I am not looking for your sympathy. I am trying to make a point. I loved both of my wives. If I had tried to write about the downward spiral toward death of either of my wives, I would have sounded negative. I fear that I am watching the downward spiral toward death of Christ's church in the United States of America. I love the church. When I sound too negative, forgive me, please. I find little room for optimism. If the church in America is as sick as the symptoms seem to indicate, I can sound positive only in those rare moments that I think of the vague possibility of recovery. Yes, miracles are possible. However, as I have said on many occasions in the marriage counseling office, "In all my years of working with couples, I have never seen God work a miracle in behalf of people who are consistenely behaving in ways counter to the ways of God." Jesus called for repentance and He demanded love (*agapé*)—the kind of love that consistently works in other people's best interests. Without repentance and a lifestyle characterized by love (*agapé*), major segments of the church in North America will die!

Some church leaders think they see room for hope. We are yet to learn if the light ahead in the tunnel is the light of a new day or the light of oncoming disaster.

Everyone who is concerned with evangelism as an integral part of the larger field of Church Growth, must study means and methods of leading people to God through His Savior-Son, Jesus the Christ. Dr. Hollis Green, a towering figure in the field of Church Growth has said that, "Men transformed by the New Testament dynamic, become a means to reach others. . . ."[2] If this author and educator is correct, perhaps the entire field of Church Growth must ask a disturbing question. Is the modern church membership really made up of "transformed men" (and women)? *Is the church expecting the unconverted (untransformed) (unregenerate) members to lead others into a saving, transformed, new birth relationship with Christ?*

Or has the church become another mission field—perhaps America's most difficult, most closed mission field. Few tasks can be more difficult to accomplish than trying to re-evangelize the evangelized. When I preached in the prison, *no man had to be persuaded* that he had been practicing sin. When I preach in a church, almost *no one wants to admit* that he or she has ever committed a specific act of sin.

When administrators in industry are forced to admit that something is wrong in their institutions, outside consultants may be invited in to help. But they do not come in from the outside equipped to tell what is wrong. They come to conduct attitude and issue surveys and intensive discussions with employees who already have clear ideas about what is wrong. Those who are a part of the institution most clearly know the truth. They also are the ones who are most likely to have clear ideas on how to improve conditions. The outside world may be in a position to point to the outward *symptoms* of the church's illness. However, only we of the church are in a position to study the symptoms closely enough to determine the *cause* of the illness, and to determine that which must happen to promote its return to good health. Many will disagree with my diagnoses and recommendations for promoting a cure in the chapters ahead. Uninformed opinion deserves no consideration. Informed opinion should be weighed carefully. Mine is informed opinion, and I will quote from those with informed opinion.

Even if you disagree, in part, with what I am seeing and proposing, cooperatively, perhaps we can arrive at a course of action that will make the modern church into the body of Christ that He intended it to be.

A friend that I met in a local supermarket asked what I was writing these days. I responded that I am working on a manuscript on sins in modern churches. A woman, not of my acquaintance ahead of me in the checkout line, unexpectedly turned and in a hushed voice said, "I can tell you one sign that something's wrong in the church today. We are investing in multi-million dollar recreational centers in our efforts to keep our young people who don't see that we have anything spiritually worthwhile to offer them. If we can't offer something spiritually worthwhile, at least we can offer something for their entertainment that will keep them in or around the church building." She turned away. I had never seen her before and have not seen her since. I would like to have been able to run after her to tell her that she was completely wrong. Instead, I paid the cashier, and as I walked to my car, I wondered to what degree the woman might be correct.

Both the Old Testament and the New Testament declare that the wages of sin is death. And the sins of a major segment of the modern church are truly deadly. The church's influence on its own members is dying. Its respect by the world is dying, and its impact for positive change on America's society is dying. At least one denomination is seeing its negative influence spilling over into its foreign mission work. Up to 80% of that denomination's mission converts are lost within two months after their baptism, and as many as 30-40% of their new converts in some missions never return to church after baptism. Denominational leaders are watching the steady decline in attendance and membership across the U.S. Some denominations that boast the greatest numbers, cannot find fifty percent of their members. They literally do not know where they are.

If we listen to the reports of the mega churches and to the voices that tell us that more than 40 percent of the population of the United States attends church worshipservices each week, we could easily conclude that all is well with the churches of America. However, for several years, some have questioned the accuracy of the glowing statistical reports. Church planter and researcher, David T. Olson, doubted reports that on any given Sunday 43 percent to 49 percent of Americans attend worship services. He believed that head count research would reveal more accurate information than that of previous researchers who had relied on interview-survey respondents. Olson suspected that many people were dishonest when asked if they had attended church during the previous weekend. He believes that people want to look good for the pollster, causing something researchers call the "halo effect"—an exaggeration beyond reality. As Director of the American Church Research Project, for roughly twenty years, Olson has led researchers to perform a head count of people entering more than 200,000 churches to compare pollster's reports with reality. He has concluded that, in truth, fewer than 20 percent of all people in the United States actually attend church on any given weekend. In 2005, only 17.5 percent did so. He further identified church attenders by religious traditions.

Of that 17.5 percent, 9.1 percent were Evangelicals, 5.3 percent were Roman Catholic, and only 3.0 percent of that 17.5 percent attended the mainline churches.[3] *These, he defines as the Episcopal Church, the Evangelical Lutheran Church, the Presbyterian Church (USA), the United Methodist church, the Christian (Disciples of Christ), and the United Church of Christ). These six mainline churches have experienced more than 40 consecutive years of membership decline. Olson has written, "As a group, these churches are projected to decline by 14 percent in numerical attendance in this decade, a loss of well over a million weekly attendees."*[4]

Baptists show some growth outside the South. However, in no Southern state is the increase in membership of Baptist churches keeping up with the rate of population increase.

Studying the rate of decline in church attendance across the United States, the American Church Research Project reports that in 1990, 20.4 percent of attended church on any given weekend. By 2005, the percentage had dropped to 18.7 percent, and to 17.5 percent by 2005. A website devoted to Olson's research reports that the number of people who attend church on any given weekend had dropped to 17 percent in 2007. Based on these and other figures that show the broader picture, this research group projects that by 2050, only 10 percent of Americans will be in church on any given Sunday.[5] *Indeed, if attendance continues to decline by half of a percentage point during each two year period as it did between 2005 and 2007, the percentage of Americans who attend worship each weekend may decline to 10 percent well before 2040! In addition to the reasons sited by Olson, in the pages ahead, we will examine seven sins that beset major segments of organized Christianity in America today.* The wages of sin is death—for nations, marriages, individuals, and even for local churches. I fear we now hear the death rattle of the church in America.

The church in America may truly die. However, from the days of Noah, God has always managed to save a remnant of persons who remained faithful. While the more theologically liberal churches and denominations watch a decline, the most theologically conservative watch a slow, but steady growth. That is not a biased opinion. That is a fact that is easy to verify.   Is the laity trying to tell the clergy something?

If the church dies in North America, God will save a remnant, but the United States' place as a strong "Christian nation" may be too near death to survive. Many voices have already referred to the United States as Post Christian America. The greatest hope for survival and fresh leadership of the Christian faith may lie in South Korea! Contrary to the thought of many minds, the world's lead for those who follow Christ could come from Russia or China. In the meantime, if the church is to survive in America, we may need to place it in an Intensive Care Unit. Perhaps the pages ahead will stimulate efforts for treatment.

I have to confess that for many years, I pretended to believe that all is well in the church. A few years ago, a friend and I sat enjoying a light lunch when he looked across the table and said, "Bill, there's something wrong with Christianity. It isn't working." Between bites of food, I mentally collected many of the good things that I have witnessed. I recalled a family of five whose lives were in chaos from alcohol abuse, and unabashed hostilities. When they surrendered their lives to the living Christ, He transformed their whole world. They were born anew and it showed. Someone has suggested, "Don't ask if a man is a Christian. Watch him. His life will tell you." I thought of many more people similar to the transformed lives I have seen. I thought of the nursing homes, the homes for unwed mothers, the hospitals, the orphanages, the food kitchens, and numerous other ministries scattered across the land. All of them serve human needs in response to God's commandment to make love a lifestyle of action that works in the best interests of others. "No, I thought to myself, Christianity is still working. Perhaps some few are not working it." But I had essentially turned him off. I reminded myself, "He has a bias against those whom he views as Fundamentalists. In brief, I dismissed his observations. But his comments began to haunt my thoughts.

A reasonably intelligent mind cannot permanently tolerate conflicting, disagreeing "facts." As a young man, beginning to study for ministry, I experienced a pivotal moment in my thought. I had joined a group of other young men who preached each week at the local jail. We needed a place to "practice our preaching." In the mid 1950s, we had life term prisoners farmed out from the South Carolina State Penitentiary to local city jails. From week to week, in the City Jail of Greenville, S.C., I found among those criminals—among those from whom society needed protection—among those men who did not need to be persuaded that they had done wrong—I found men I liked. I found little sham and pretence. I found men who accepted Christ's message that called for repentance and offered the grace of forgiveness and regeneration. However, it also was there that I had an experience that screamed, "Something's wrong!"

Among those life-term prisoners in the city jail, were also drunks from off the street who were in for an overnight lock-up. (We were not permitted to mingle with them. Iron bars separated us.) One evening, a drunk stumbled to the bars, and held on to keep from falling. In the midst of my sermon, he yelled, "I don't need to hear what you've got to say, preacher! I was saved back there some thirty-five years ago and, praise God, once saved—always saved!" As he yelled the last words, he slid down the bars, lost consciousness, and lay in a heap at my feet. I stood in surprised silence.

Somewhere inside, a voice screamed, "Something's wrong here! He thinks he's 'saved' but from all appearances, he's as lost as a man in the middle of the ocean in a canoe without a paddle or a compass. He doesn't have to wait for Hell. He's already suffering in a corner of it and doesn't even know it!" Here at my feet lay a man who had walked the aisle of a church in years gone by. He had filled out a form, had said the right words to the preacher, but had walked out of the church unrepentant and unregenerate, having tried to accept Christ his Savior without having accepted Christ as Lord of his life.

Another pivotal moment in my thinking occurred many years later during follow-up research to a doctoral dissertation. I had performed a ground breaking study of the development of perceptions of the personality of God among the general population, and was replicating the study among prisoners in the Tennessee State Prison system. I discovered that of the men who enter Brushy Mountain (Tennessee's Maximum Security Prison), more than 95% profess themselves to be Christians. What? Something's wrong! It is possible that they were lying. It is also possible that something is wrong with those men's perception of Christianity. On the other hand, perhaps something is wrong with my research instrument. I reviewed it again and recalled that the research instrument had tested positively. A professional statistician at the University of Tennessee had examined my research instrument. My Graduate Committee at Oxford Graduate School had scrutinized my research quite closely, and had even given me an award for the research. Still disbelieving the evidence, I called the prison chaplain and expressed my dismay.

"Bill, there's nothing wrong with your research. I've known for several years that about 95% of the men who come here claim to be Christians when we process them in."

He did not tell me that the figures are similar all over the United States!

Those of us who are members of a church tend to be proud of our church. We form friendships, and think of one another as brothers and sisters in the faith. Occasionally, we see or learn of fellow members who are consistently living entirely contrary to the teachings of Jesus Christ, our Lord. We feel disappointed, even saddened. We may even wonder, "How can Christians act like that?" If we secretly suspect they may not truly be Christians, we feel guilty, telling ourselves that we should not make such judgments; we should leave judgment to God. We may even quote the words of Jesus to ourselves, "Judge not, and ye shall not be judged. . ." (Lk. 6:37). We will leave each person to hear the judgment of God as God chooses to speak. Judgment may be harsh for those that "profess that they know God; but in works they deny him" (Titus1:16). Speaking of judgment, Jesus warned that He would declare, "Depart from me, ye that work iniquity."

While we try not to judge, we may remember other words of Jesus, "By their fruits ye shall know them" (Matthew 7:20). Although God has not called us to serve as "fruit inspectors," some "fruit" is so good and some is so bad that its quality is obvious to people both inside and outside the church. When I worked in a peach packing shed in South Carolina during my youth, some fruit was so rotten that its condition was obvious to anyone who glanced at it. Most was good and sound.

Any *honest* assessment must recognize some of the most honorable, honest, loving, caring, and noble souls on earth make up a large segment of the church. However, at the same time any *honest* assessment must recognize that some of the most dishonorable, dishonest, unloving, uncaring, and ignoble souls on earth also make up a segment of the church. Both, those who are outside the church and those within the church observe the evidence that declares, "Something's wrong."

Even a superficial reading of the New Testament makes clear that followers of Jesus are expected to be a different people—so different that they are required to be born anew—from above to gain citizenship in the Kingdom of God. Lives of Christ's early followers were so changed—so patterned—

so modeled after their Lord that those who knew them began to call them Christians. They admired those early Christian's moral/ethical behavior. They were the "people of the way"—the people who lived the lifestyle of Jesus the Christ.

However, as we prepare to enter the second decade of the twenty-first century, the world is not seeing people called "Christians"—people of the church as people who live the lifestyle of Jesus. They see the people of the church living in the same sin as everyone else—or worse.

In the counseling office, when my counselees began to feel angry, we usually were getting close to some painful truth that the counselee did not want to admit.

While reading this book, if you find yourself becoming angry with me, I would encourage you to pause for deep reflection. That which offends you most may be that which you most need to heed. Do not base your judgement of what I say on the teachings of your denomination, your church doctrine, your personal beliefs, or on the beliefs of your spiritual leader. Base your judgement solely of the Bible, God's written Word. Turn to your Bible and read sited passages within their context.

Unless otherwise noted, scriptural quotations are from the King James Version of the Bible. Numbered end-notes are available on the closing pages of this book.

Although I am indebted to my daughter, Lisa Justice Montgomery, to educators and friends, Spencer and Becky Hudson, to the Rev. Dr. William (Bill) Cope, a dear friend for more than forty years, and to fellow members of the Heart of the Valley Writers Guild for their suggestions for improvement of the manuscript, I alone stand responsible for the final product.

SIN 1
THE FOUNDATIONAL SIN:
FAILURE TO SUBMIT TO JESUS THE
CHRIST

And he said to them all,
If any man will come after me,
let him deny himself,
and take up his cross daily,
and follow me. Luke 9:23

Stop! Did you read the Introduction?
It is crucial for all that follows.

Much of the modern church has failed to accept and to promote one of the most elementary tenets of the Christian faith: Jesus is the Christ; the Messiah; the King. In daily conversation, we may speak of Jesus, or of Christ, or we may speak of Jesus Christ. In a culture that has thoroughly integrated the language of the Christian faith, we use all three ways of referring to Jesus as if all three were His name. Indeed, many people who have been members of the church for many years assume that Jesus Christ is His first and last name.

In the first century Mediterranean world, few men carried a sir name. A male was often identified by his home-town. Jesus was often called "Jesus of Nazareth," and we may have read of Saul of Tarsus, or "Joseph of Arimathaea." However, more often men were referred to as the son of his father or the son of the man known for his craft. Therefore, in Nazareth, the small, insignificant village of eighty to one hundred houses and three hundred to five hundred residents, Jesus probably was known as Jesus Bar (son of) Joseph, or Jesus Bar

Carpenter. Christ was the identifying title of His adult role as God's Savior-King whose coming had been foretold for many hundreds of years.

For more than a thousand years before Jesus' birth, the Jews had used the title "King" and "Anointed One" *completely interchangeably.* A newly proclaimed king might have enjoyed having someone place a crown or golden war-helmet on his head. He also might have enjoyed receiving a costly breastplate with magnificent jewels, and mounds of gold and silver, but these were only signs of his having been named as the people's king. Kingship was created only by *the oil that was poured over his head* from a vile. His head was *anointed.* Saul had been the first man anointed as king over those loosely knit tribes who later became known as Jews.

The Hebrew word for "to anoint" was *mashah,* and "the Anointed One" was called the *Mashih.* When that word was translated into the European languages fifteen hundred years after Jesus' birth, it became "Messiah." Unlike the Old Testament which was written in the Hebrew language, the New Testament was written in Greek. The word "Messiah" when translated into the Greek language becomes, "Christ." In the briefest statement, the word "Messiah" and the word "Christ" mean precisely the same. They both refer to God's anointed King over His people.

After King Saul's death in battle, David was anointed king, and he slowly forged twelve loosely connected tribes into a mighty flourishing nation. Future generations would look back on David's reign as their "Golden Age." After David had died, the warring forces of Assyria, Persia and Babylon tromped repeatedly through the land of Palestine. Then marched the Greeks, who were followed by the Romans. During those terribly troubled times, the prophets began foretelling of the coming of a just and pious king, an "Anointed One," a "Messiah." Micah had added to the prophecies and even predicted that the Messiah (the Christ) would arrive in Bethlehem as an infant born of a virgin. The Prophet Isaiah had written:

> For unto us a child is born, unto us a son is given: and the government shall be upon his shoulder: and his name shall be called Wonderful Counselor, The Mighty God, The everlasting Father, The Prince of Peace (Isa. 9:6).

Isaiah further prophesied that this child, upon whose shoulder the government would rest (as king), would be "The Mighty God" in human flesh (God incarnated). He would not be one limited to hold only God's authority, He would be the embodiment of God Himself. God Himself would take on the form of an earthly King. The King, the Anointed One, the Messiah was coming in human flesh! He was "the Hope of Israel." This is the direction to which virtually every Jewish mind turned at the mention of the Messiah. He would take the throne of Israel, and ultimately would rule the whole world from that throne.

By the time Jesus was born, Romans had occupied the Jew's beloved "Promised Land," Palestine, for more than sixty years. The regional kings, acting in behalf of Rome, held the people under oppression. Before Jesus arrived, more than one hundred fifty thousand Jews had died in revolutionary efforts to overthrow the shackles of the Roman Empire. During the days of His flesh, the air was electric with revolutionary promotions among the people.

About the time Jesus was born, a formidable body of Galileans rose in armed revolt against their Roman rulers. It climaxed in Sepphoris, only three and a half miles from Nazareth, with the crucifixion of two thousand insurgents. Thousands of others were taken away into slavery.

A second major revolt against Rome ignited when Jesus was roughly eleven about which the New Testament seems to give only a hint (cf. Luke 13:1). It, too, climaxed near Nazareth with a terrible slaughter of Romans and Galileans by the sword, followed with the crucifixion of another 2000 men, and more were taken as slaves. Some non-Biblical sources leave room to suspect that Mary's father may have been among those crucified at the end of one of those two uprisings and her mother could have been sold into slavery.

Believing that God would save them from the Romans, virtually every Jew expected God to deliver them from their oppressors by sending His deliverer-king, the Messiah.

The Pharisees sited their interpretations of more than 450 references to the Messiah within the Torah (the Biblical books of Genesis, Exodus, Leviticus, Numbers, and Deuteronomy). They sited more than 240 additional references in the writings of the Prophets and supported those with more than 550 references to the Messiah in their most ancient rabbinic writings.

The first recorded account of Jesus' claim to be the long awaited Messiah was made as He journeyed through Samaria where He encountered the "woman at the well" (John 4:6-42). The Samaritans, a "mixed-breed" of people with remnants of Jewish blood flowing through their veins held Messianic expectations similar to the expectations of the Jews.

In addition to the Jewish expectations of a Redeemer King,[6] virtually all the known world held similar beliefs.

Even some prominent Romans shared the spirit of anticipation that awaited the rise of a great king from out of Judea. Plutarch reported stories of the people's dismay at learning of the death of the great god, Pan.[7] New Testament historian, David Smith added, "Such stories—and there are many—reveal what despair had filled men's hearts when Jesus came. It seemed as though the world's sun had set and its night was hastening on. . . even the heathen were turning eyes toward Judea, thence expecting their deliverer."[8]

Tacitus, speaking of his Romans said, "People are generally persuaded in the faith of the ancient prophesies, that the East was to prevail, and that from Judea was to come the Master and Ruler of the world." Suetonius, in his account of the life of Vespasian said, "It was an old and constant belief throughout the East, that by indubitably certain prophecies, the Jews were to attain the highest power. . . ." "Out of Judah would come 'mastery over the world.'"

Even among the Greeks, during their troubled times Aeschylus wrote, "Look not for any end, moreover, to this curse until God appears, to accept upon His Head the pangs of thy own sins vicarious." Cicero wrote about a "King whom we must recognize to be saved." The Fourth Eclogue of Virgil, after writing of the same belief, spoke of "a chaste woman, smiling on her infant boy, with whom the iron-age would pass away." He also spoke of a forthcoming golden child "filled with the life of the gods" who would bring in a kingdom of love, where the sins of humankind would fade away.[9]

Sages in China, writing from the Far East, anticipated a great Wise Man who would arise from their west: "In the 24th year of Tchao-Wang of the dynasty of the Tcheou, on the 8th day of the 4th moon, a light appeared in the Southwest which illumined the king's palace. The monarch, struck by its splendor, interrogated the sages. They showed him books in which this prodigy signified the appearance of the great Saint of the West whose religion was to be introduced into this country."

In the course of world history, many men have been declarer to be gods, but never before in history has the coming of a god been foretold for hundreds of years, by peoples from throughout the known inhabited world.

In far away Persia, men wrote of their expectations of a great king who would rise out of Judea and rule the world. It was there, that students of the movement of heavenly bodies, spied a bright new star in the western sky. History sometimes refers to these astronomers (astrologers?) as "Magi" and at others as "Wise men"—philosophers and scientists—followers of Zoroastrianism – a creed that opposed the worship of graven images, and believed that there was only one God who should be worshiped by all persons.

Not from India, the land of the origin of Hinduism and Buddhism, or from China, the origin of Confucianism, or from Persia, the origin of Islam, were men looking for redemption. Men were expecting their salvation to come from Judea. This coming Savior-King was known among the Jews as the Messiah – among the Greeks and Romans as the Christ.

In the modern world, most of us are too far removed from kings and queens to comprehend their role in ancient history. In the first century, everyone in the civilized world, and many in the not so civilized world, understood precisely the power and role of a king.

A king was the absolute ruler over all who dwelled within the boundaries of his domain – his realm—his land—his kingdom. It was *his* kingdom. It belonged to *him*. Everyone clearly understood that citizens were "subjects" of the king. *They were "subject" to the king's authority and "subjects" were expected to serve the king.*

Representative government had no place in the mind of the king. Laws of the land were created, not by a body of the citizens, but by the king—usually in keeping with his best interests! His army stood behind him as enforcers of his law. When the king sent forth his word, either by written proclamation, or by a personal representative who spoke his word, he expected obedience. Whether his words were spoken by a representative or written on parchment, the hearers knew the words came with the same authority as if the voice of the king had spoken to them face to face.

When a king went forth in war, he went to force the people into subjugation. The conquered became his subjects—his servants—without regard to their desires. However, he was his people's protector. The king might oppress his own people, but they were safe from oppression by any other power. His scepter symbolized the shepherd's rod of protection against enemies.

The king could make his people into absolute slaves, if he chose to do so. He became their "lord." He became their "master." Those forced into his kingdom were forced to submit (bow) themselves to his rule.

In 333 B.C., Darius, King of Persia and most of the known world, prepared for war. He had not learned that it is as disastrous to over-estimate one's own ability as it is to under-estimate the ability of one's enemy. Darius took his wife, son, and mother along to watch the sport of battle against a brazen young upstart called Alexander the Great with an army of only 40,000 men. Darius led 100,000 experienced warriors. Most wars of that period were fought during the daylight hours of one day. By the end of the day, the combined losses of the two armies totaled approximately 100,000 men. Darius' routed troops had scattered to the four winds, and Darius had fled on horseback to hide in the nearby mountains.

Alexander took Darius' family under his protection and sent a messenger to tell Darius that he could have them back if he would bow and submit to Alexander as his king. Darius would rather leave his mother, wife, and son as hostages, and he would rather die than to humbly surrender and pledge

5

allegiance to Alexander. Surrender and acceptance of Alexander as his ruler was unthinkable.

Darius was not unlike millions of Americans who would rather die in their sin than to surrender to the leadership of Christ. And many of them hold prominent positions in local churches across the land. Many are afraid that if they surrender their will to the will of God, they will lose their own identity. Others simply cannot tolerate the thought of bowing in recognition of any authority above themselves. Many, would never say the words, but by their actions they say, "I don't want or need anybody, even God, telling me what to do or how to live my life. I know what's best for me!" (Is this not the essence of the attitude of Adam and Eve?) The "American way" of prideful independence accepts no ruling authority. Many feel that they must be in absolute control while at the same time their lives show evidence that they are living completely out of their own control.

During the thirty-one years I served as a bedside hospital chaplain, I listened to hundreds who boasted in one moment of their independence and then watched them weep a few minutes later about the chaos of their lives and the pain they had brought upon themselves. Many had awakened to the fact that they had become enslaved to some form of self-defeating, self-destructive habit of the heart.[10] As if the "natural" resistance to authority were not strong enough, we have glorified the "rugged individualist" who wants or needs no one. We have glorified the person who breaks his way through the wilderness without compass or guide. One of the most popular singers of the twentieth century, in his later years arrogantly crooned that he was not among those who had bowed or kneeled before any authority (God was clearly implied). He boasted of having lived, "My Way." He had accepted no Compass or Guide. His song spoke for millions.

Although both, men and women are inclined to resist authority, a gender factor appears to be active in decisions to submit to the authority of God's rule in life. A view of the congregation of almost any church will reveal a disproportionate number of women as compared to the number of men. Historically, it has seemed more natural for a woman to surrender to a male (God is represented in the Bible as the Father and Jesus is male) than for a man to surrender to a man. One man spoke for many, "I'm afraid that if I surrender to God, I'll lose my manhood." (Yes, even Freudianism slips into the side door of the church.) Darius was not the first or the last of those who would rather give up almost anything of value than to accept another as a higher authority than themselves.

Two years after the initial bloody battle between the armies of Darius and Alexander, the two armies clashed again. That day became the bloodiest day in history, rivaling the number of deaths by the Atomic bomb at Hiroshima.

At the end of the one-day battle of Arbela, three hundred thousand men lay dead, and a near-equal amount of torn and bleeding flesh laid in dead horses and elephants.)

Although most subjects were forced to submit to the rule of ancient kings, people from other lands (other kingdoms) could voluntarily enter a kingdom and thereby submit to the king's rule with expectations to live by his law. They accepted that king was their Lord. He was their Master.

All of this was clearly in the minds of the people when Jesus invited them to enter the Kingdom of God. They were intimately aware of what it meant to live under a king. They knew that a King was "Lord" and "Master" of all citizens of the kingdom. When Jesus laid out the style of life expected of those who submitted themselves as subjects of the King of the Kingdom of God, the masses turned away. Many of His followers also turned away. His expectations too high.

Unlike other kings, Jesus never *forced* anyone to submit to His rule. *All* who entered His kingdom, the Kingdom of Heaven, came one by one, as through a turnstile, voluntarily bowing in submission to His rule. None became citizens of His kingdom because they lived in a holy land, or belonged to a family of believers, or had been baptized, or because they had joined as members of some religious group. Each came trusting God as the sole Ruler of his or her life.

The Jesus we know as the Christ is the king for whom the Jews waited for centuries. We Christians generally have faulted the Jews for not having accepted Jesus as their Messiah, (their Christ) their Lord. However, many in modern North America who profess to be Christians fail to accept Him as the King to whom they obediently surrender their lives.

Jesus wanted to keep on influencing their lives so that they might stand as righteous before God. To accomplish this, He needed to live within them. Therefore, they needed to invite Him into their lives. John, one of Jesus' inner circle of disciples quoted Jesus as having said that He stands knocking, waiting to be invited to enter the door of the heart (cf. Rev. 3:20). While inviting a crowd to follow Him, He told them they needed to take Him—to absorb Him into their lives. He referred to Himself as the "Living Bread" that came down from Heaven, and that by eating thereof, one would never die (cf. Jn 6:48-50). He went on to say," I [Myself] am this Living Bread and came down from heaven. If anyone eats this Bread he will live forever; and also the Bread that I shall give for the life of this world is My flesh (body). . . . you cannot have any life in you unless you eat the flesh of the Son of Man and drink His blood [unless you appropriate His life and the saving merit of His blood]. He who feeds on my flesh and drinks My blood has (possession now) eternal life, and I will raise him up [from the dead] on the last day. . .

. He who feeds on My flesh and drinks my blood dwells continually in Me, and I [in like manner dwell continually] in him" (Jn 6:51-56). This was so important in our behalf that He ceremonialized it in the final hours before His crucifixion. He established the Eucharist (Communion) (Lord's Supper) wherein with bread and wine, we symbolically incorporate His body and blood into our lives. He knew that microscopic parts of the bread and wine ultimately permeated the entire body.

By dwelling within us, he could guide (lead—not force) to control the tongue and the words it speaks. He could guide the hands in good works for those around us and for Himself. He could guide the wholesome use of the reproductive organs for sexual intercourse only within the bonds of marriage. He could guide the use of the feet to carry us to places to serve Him through serving others. By accepting His leadership, we would be accepting responsibility for our own behavior. Living obediently to this guiding influence, we would be truly accepting Him, trusting Him as our Lord.

Talk is cheap. We may *call* Him Christ while refusing to bow before Him as our king. We may *call* Him Lord while refusing to submit to His Lordship. Indeed, during the days of His flesh Jesus asked on at least one occasion, "Why do you call Me, Lord, Lord, and do not (practice) what I tell you (Luke 6:46)?" In essence, He was saying, "You waste your breath by calling me Lord when you don't obey me. Your behavior belies your words. You are still subject (obedient) to the Evil One. You are his subject, not mine. He is your lord – not I"

Those who obey Satan and blindly expect a reward of eternal Heavenly bliss seem never to have listened to Jesus when He said, "Not every one that saith unto me, Lord, Lord, shall enter into the kingdom of heaven; but *he that doeth the will of my Father* which is in heaven. Many will say to me in that day, Lord, Lord, have we not prophesied in thy name? and in thy name have cast out devils? and in thy name done many wonderful works? And then will I profess unto them, I *never knew you: depart from me, ye that **work iniquity***" (Matthew 7:21-23). (Emphases mine)

What iniquity (sin, evil)?

Theft! Robbery! Rape! Murder! Greed! Selfishness! Gossip! And hundreds of lesser misdeeds that diminish the quality of life for one's self and/or for one's neighbor!

PROFESSORS OF CHRISTIANITY PACK OUR PRISONS

Look who's packing the prisons across America. After I learned that approximately 95% of all inmates confined in Tennessee's maximum security prison profess themselves to be Christian at the time of entry, I looked further.

A recent survey in Massachusetts found every prison inmate to be "religious." In Joliet Prison, Catholic inmates numbered 2,888, Baptists numbered 1,020, Methodists included 617, and 100% of all others considered themselves to be "religious." Notorious Sing-Sing confined 1,553 prisoners. Of them, 855 were Catholics, 518 were Protestants 117 were Jews, and only 8 were non-religious. During a recent 10 year period, at Sing-Sing, of those executed for murder 65% were Catholic, 26% were Protestants, Jews 6% and less than 1/3 of 1% were non-religious.

We have been taught that *Christians are expected to live by a higher moral/ ethical code than non-Christians.* God's written word commands it. We are expected to live by the love code of Jesus. Something's wrong! A recent study found that the state of Michigan had 82,000 Baptists and 110,000 Jews. However, 22 times more Baptists are confined in Michigan prisons than Jews, and 18 times more Methodists in Michigan prisons than Jews!

Something's wrong when approximately 97% of all the inmates confined in prisons in the United States claim to be Christians on the day they arrive in prison.

Are they all lying? Or are they deceived?

Do they believe they are Christians without having surrendered to the rule of the Christ—the King? Early in the twenty-first century, Berna Research tells us that one third of all people in the U.S. claim to be "born again" Christians.

Has the church contributed to the delusion that Christian Faith is disassociated from obedience to its Christ? Has the church contributed to the belief that Christian faith is simply the belief that a series of events described in the Gospels actually happened? Has the modern church contributed to the damnation of its members by giving false assurance to its members who live in open rebellion against Jesus Christ? Or have we contributed to the belief that "believing in Jesus" is simply a mental assent to the belief that He lived as a real person in history and/or the belief in the fact that He died on a cross? Many have been deluded into believing that the academic belief in the historical reality of certain events in Jesus' life amounts to "saving faith." Is mental belief in a series of events in Jesus' life to be called, "believing in Jesus?" Is a mere belief in the truth of some facts about Jesus to be considered, "trusting Jesus as Savior?" *It is not* – if we depend on the New Testament for a definition of "believing in" Jesus or anyone else.

FAITH AS A LIFESTYLE OF OBEDIENCE

The words "believe in," "faith," "trust," and "to obey" all are closely related. In the language of the New Testament, from which these words are translated, they all come from two etymologically closely related words, *peitho* and *pisteuo. Peitho* means to obey. And *pisteuo* means to trust. Obedience (*peitho*) is a response to trust (*pisteuo*).

Many years ago, my children were instrumental in helping me understand this profoundly important truth. We had arrived at our vacation site on the Cumberland Plateau of East Tennessee. We had never visited there before. Lisa, our seven year old daughter, and David, our four year old son jumped out of the car and began running toward the wooded area behind the cabin. I called for them to wait for me. I assured Ann, my wife, that I would help unload the car after I surveyed the area for possible hazards to the children. I had heard of the magnificently carved sandstone gorges with sheer drop-offs of more than a hundred feet. I imagined a ravine beyond the edge of the woods behind the cabin.

With a gleeful youngster tugging at a finger of each hand, we walked toward the woodland while I watched for broken glass and other things in the yard that could harm the children. Before we got to the edge of the woods, I spotted a thriving patch of poison ivy nestled at the foundation of the cabin.

The three of us squatted while I explained the difference between this ivy and the ivy growing around a tree in our yard back home. I warned them that if they touched this ivy, it would hurt them. They would not feel any discomfort immediately, but within a few hours, they would feel miserable. I explained that wherever their skin touched those shiny dark green leaves, little red bumps would appear that would soon turn into little blisters that would itch terribly. ("It will itch like crazy," was my "daddy talk" description.) After we had wandered over the whole yard and into the woodland behind the cabin, I opened the door and paused. I looked back to the children and called out, "We are going to be here for several days. Have fun. Play in the yard, but stay away from that patch of poison ivy near the back of the cabin."

Only later, did I realize that we had re-enacted events analogous to those in the Garden of Eden. God had given Adam and Eve the Garden of Eden as a place to enjoy their lives. They could eat freely of all the trees except one. Something about the fruit of that tree would harm them. They had understood that God wanted them neither to eat nor to touch the fruit of the tree in the midst of the garden (Genesis 3:2-3).

Lisa and David had never seen poison ivy before that time. My word was their only basis for judging it harmful. They had no experience with poison ivy. Each one had to make an independent decision. Each one could decide, "I will do what I want to, when I want to do it. I will trust my own judgment over my daddy's." And without any punishment by me, they would have suffered the natural consequences of their disobedience. Or independently, they each could decide, "My daddy wants what's best for me. I don't know by personal experience that I will be harmed by the pretty shiny leaves, but

I'm going to do as he told me. I trust him enough to obey him. I'll trust his judgment over my own." By trusting me, they were *saved* from the discomfort of poison ivy's itching blisters. Even the Apostle Paul recognized that there is a sense in which we "work out our own salvation" (cf. Philippians 2:12).

They each decided to trust me enough to do as I had instructed. They *believed in me* enough to obey me. (I am not suggesting that they always did so.)

The person who truly believes in Jesus will obey Him! Faith shows itself in obedient behavior. There is no saving faith without obedience to the Savior. Virtually every person who has professed Christianity has memorized John 3:16. "For God so loved the world that He gave His only begotten Son, that whosoever believeth in Him should not perish, but have everlasting life." The word "believe," as used here is synonymous with the word "obey."

Every evangelist who has ever walked into a pulpit has used that verse of Scripture to invite listeners to be saved. Unfortunately, many have responded believing that the words "believe in" call for a momentary academic belief that will assure them of "eternal life." They have not understood that **believing in Him is equal to obeying Him**. And **disobedience is equal to unbelief**. Those who would merely profess to believe without obedience object to the words of Jesus as recorded in John 3:36. "He that believeth on the Son hath eternal life; but he that *obeyeth not* the Son shall not see life, but *the wrath of God abideth on him."* (Italics added) The writer of Hebrews picked up on Jesus' warning when he wrote, "And to whom was God talking when he promised that they would never enter his rest? He was talking to those who did not *obey* him. So we see they were not allowed to enter and have God's rest, because they did not *believe"* (Hebrews 3:18-19). Emphasis mine.

The word faith in the Scripture repeatedly refers to a *continuing activity*. Saving faith is proclaimed by the Greek verb, *pisteuo* (keep on believing). Throughout his account of the Gospel, John used this present tense of the word "believe." (cf. John 3:14-18, 36; 5:24; 6:35, 40, 47; 7:38; 11:25-26; 12:44, 46; and 20:31. Also Acts 10:43, 13:39; Romans 1:16, 3:22; 4:5; 9:33; 10:4, 10-11). *All* of these passages, including John 3:16, were written in the present (ongoing, ongoing, ever-present) tense. If the intent had been to make the phrase "believe in" a one-time, or non-enduring event, the New Testament (Greek) writers would have used the aorist tense of the verb.

Anyone who reflects for more than a moment recognizes that the ongoing nature of "believing in Jesus" speaks directly to the theological doctrine of "eternal security of the believer." (Note that I did not use the oft-repeated phrase, "Once saved, always saved." There is a difference.) The person who *goes on believing* (trusting, obeying) is eternally secure. The person who goes on trusting enough to keep on obeying, keeps on being secure.) Faith that is momentary, short-lived or temporary—faith that was only a recollection of an event in one's personal history is unknown as saving faith in the New Testament. The New Testament knows only of ongoing, active faith that is demonstrated by turning away from the ongoing practice of disobedience to the ways of God to ongoing obedience to God, the King. The New Testament uses the word "walk" as a way of encouraging Christians to follow an ongoing lifestyle. No fewer than 96 times does it insist that we keep on "walking," (regulating our lives, conducting ourselves, passing our lives) in humble obedience to God.

The Apostle Paul wrote to the Galatians, "The acts of the sinful nature are obvious: sexual immorality, impurity, debauchery (repetitive, loveless, cheap sex); idolatry and witchcraft; hatred, discord, jealousy, fits of rage, selfish ambition, dissensions, factions and envy; drunkenness, orgies, and the like, I warn you, as I did before, that those who live like this *will not inherit the kingdom of God*" (Gal. 5:19-21 NIV Italics mine). Following those words, Paul stated that "those who belong to Christ Jesus have nailed the passions and desires of their sinful nature to his cross and crucified them there." (Gal. 5:24 NLT).

How have we of the church left room for many to conclude that "believing in Jesus" is essential, while obeying the Father is optional? Is it possible that we have so overly emphasized "salvation by God's grace" that we have *de*-emphasized the necessity obedience to Him? Or have we sometimes tried to make Christianity easy for fear of failing to add to our numbers to report at the next conference? Following the words of Paul as quoted in the prior paragraph, he wrote, "But the fruit of the Spirit is love, joy, peace, patience, kindness, goodness, faithfulness, gentleness and self control" (Gal. 5:22-23).

Of course, when Paul wrote those words, he was writing on the larger subject of the people's dependency on salvation by God's grace as compared to efforts to gain salvation by living obediently to the Jewish Law. If our motive for obeying God is to attain His salvation, we would never be "good enough" to gain salvation.

He was saying that although we are saved by God's grace, our obedience to Him is motivated by our determination to surrender to His Lordship—His rule over our lives as our King/Messiah/Christ. After having faithfully surrendered to the Lordship of the King, He extends His grace of forgiveness, reconciles us unto Himself, and recreates the new citizen of the kingdom of God who fervently works to obey the King.

SALVATION ALWAYS BY THE GRACE OF GOD
Surely, anyone who has seriously studied the Bible must recognize that salvation in both the Old Testament and New Testament always has been

identical. ***All salvation is and always has been by the grace of God.*** Even Abram (Abraham) found Jehovah to be gracious. ". . . he believed in (trusted, was obedient to) the Lord; and He counted it to him for righteousness (the Lord declared him righteous because of his faith" (Genesis 15:16 KJV & NLB).

Every other religion in human history has taught that those who were adequately obedient to the god would be accepted by the god. In effect, they have taught that every person must save himself. However, the whole Bible is a record of God's effort to gain the obedience of humankind, not for His sake, but for the benefit of humankind. He has always demanded repentance and a commitment to obediently follow His path of righteousness. Those who did so, God graciously saved while forgiving their sin (their *un*righteousness)[11] . In the same way men have trusted God for salvation, Jesus called for them to trust him. He said, "You believe in God. Believe also in me" (John 14:1) He was saying, "You trust God. Trust me also." On another occasion He said, "I and the Father are one." He was not saying that they were merely in accord with one another. Their very nature, essence, and power were one (cf. John 10:30).

Jesus said, "He who believeth on (trusts) the Son hath everlasting life: and he that believeth not (trusts not) shall not see life; but the wrath of God abideth on him" (John 3:36). The Amplified Bible translates that verse: "And he who believes in (has faith in, clings to, relies on) the Son has (now possesses) eternal life. But whoever disobeys (is unbelieving toward, refuses to trust in, disregards, is not subject to) the Son will never see (experience) life,[12] but (instead) the wrath of God abides on him. (God's displeasure remains on him; His indignation hangs over him continually.")

The Gospel, as Jesus presented it, is a "complete Gospel." The Gospel according to Jesus requires a balance. It requires no less emphasis on God's grace but an equal emphasis on obedience to Him.

The Apostle Paul continued the message of Jesus by saying that he wanted his ministry to result in obedience to Christ by word and deed (cf. Romans 15:18). In Romans 16:26 he wrote of "the obedience of faith." The writer of Hebrews continued showing the inseparability of faith in Jesus and deeds of obedience to Him (the Christ). "And being made perfect, he became the author of eternal salvation unto all them that obey him" (Hebrews 5:9). In Hebrews 11:8, the writer recognized that *by faith* Abraham *obeyed* God. Paul wrote to Titus about those who were defiled and unbelieving as men who professed to know God but by their disobedience, they denied Him (cf. Titus 1:15-16). If they practiced disobedience, Jesus was not truly their Christ; their Savior-King. They deluded themselves if they believed they were citizens of God's kingdom when they conducted their lives more consistent with citizenship in the kingdom of Satan.

The church that does not urgently promote a trusting, obedient, ongoing submission to the rule of the Christ—the Messiah—the anointed one—the King, is falling short (sinning). Furthermore, the sin is resulting in deadly consequences.

The earliest known declaration of Christian faith recognized Jesus the Christ as Lord. Within a few years after Jesus' crucifixion, resurrection, and ascension, Jesus' followers were considered a new Jewish sect known as the Nazarenes. Those Nazarenes soon became known also as "Christians."

By the end of the first century they had adopted the fish as a symbol of their faith. Their most foundational statement of faith was simple: "Jesus is the Christ, the Son of God, and my Savior." The Greek words for that statement are *Iesous Christos Theou Yios Soter.* When they formed an acrostic from those words, they spelled *ichthys* (IXΘΥΣ) which is the Greek word for "fish."

When early Christians came under persecution, this symbol, the fish sometimes was used as a secret sign to identify one another. They were declaring their faith that Jesus, before whom they submitted as their Christ (King/Messiah) the Lord, was the Son of God, and as such they knew Him to be their Savior.

When the church urges men to enter Heaven by the grace of God, we must not fail to urge them to live under the ruling lordship of the King of the Kingdom of Heaven. Blessed are those who are urging men and women and boys and girls to surrender themselves to the rule of the Messiah (Christ), and inviting them to live out their days on earth as subjects of the Kingdom of Heaven.

Is not the church contributing to the eternal damnation of those who enter her doors without becoming clearly informed? All who enter must hear that *the Christian faith demands submissive, ongoing obedience to God who revealed Himself most fully in His Christ (the Messiah/Anointed One) the King of the Kingdom of God.*

Or does the modern church really believe that the Messiah came in the person of Jesus? Having listened to many hundreds of sermons—having listened to many hundreds of persons behind the closed doors of the professional counseling office—and having listened at the bedside of thousands of persons during thirty-one years of hospital chaplaincy, I see a mountain of evidence pointing to the negative. The evidence I have seen tells me that the overwhelming majority of persons influenced by modern Christianity maintain an Old Testament perception of the nature of God.

The popular language says that they view the nature of God as if Jesus, His most complete revelation of Himself had never lived on planet Earth.

OLD TESTAMENT IMAGE OF GOD IN THE NEW TESTAMENT ERA

Two thousand years into *this Post-Incarnation Era, North Americans live with the Pre-Incarnation view of God.* Although God came revealing Himself in the person of Jesus the Christ, most North Americans of the Judeo-Christian heritage yet view God as if Jesus had never lived on planet Earth. Instead of looking to the New Testament to understand the nature of God, even active worshippers in the church still tend to be frozen with the Old Testament image.

Even seminary-trained ministers of the Gospel of Jesus Christ are inclined to hold an Old Testament view of God instead of a New Testament view. A pastor to whom I listened regularly during a period of my life preached fewer than ten percent of his sermons from the New Testament. He once preached for more than a year without delivering a message from the words of Jesus. However, he viewed himself as a "minister of the Gospel." Listeners had to strain to find any hint of "Good News'" (Gospel) in his sermons. He could have preached most of his sermons if God had never become enfleshed in the person of Jesus of Nazareth. When the clergy fails to recognize the personality of God as revealed in Jesus, it is little wonder that the masses cling to an Old Testament perception of God. With notable exceptions, the Old Testament and the New Testament present a very DIFFERENT IMAGE OF GOD!

Although the words I am about to relate may or may not be true, they illustrate an important point. On her way home from Sunday School, a little girl was reported to have said, "Mama, I like Jesus, but I don't like that angry, ol' mean God." Even a child can see a vast difference between the image of God portrayed as understood by the writers of the Old Testament in comparison to the image of God revealed in the New Testament! If we are really honest, we may be inclined to agree with the little girl. God, as he was understood in the Old Testament often is not presented as a very likeable Person.

Within the last 24 hours, I was reading of a minister who asked a man if he believed in God. The man replied, "What god are you talking about? Tell me about the nature of the god you have in mind, and I will tell you whether I believe in him."

JESUS REVEALS GOD'S TRUE NATURE

If we want to know what God is like, we can look at Jesus Christ, God's Son, as revealed in the New Testament. Jesus came as God in the flesh—God's fullest revelation of Himself. One who knew Him best called Him "the Word of God" (John 1:1-14). The written or spoken word is one of humankind's most effective means of communication. When God determined that the time was right to most totally reveal to us what He was *really* like, He gave us His enfleshed (incarnated) Word—Jesus—His most complete communication (revelation) of Himself to humankind.

Any image of God that is not in keeping with the person of Jesus Christ is a false image. Among the reasons God came in the flesh was to help destroy humankind's false images of Himself.

JESUS, THE PERFECT, COMPLETE IMAGE OF GOD

Jesus is more than just a good man and a brilliant teacher. He is a person of pre-history, and will yet live when the last word has been written by the last historian. If God truly broke into history by taking on human flesh in the person of Jesus the Christ can we not better understand God by looking at Jesus? One of Jesus' closest and most faithful followers (disciples) said of Him, "In the beginning was the Word, and the Word was with God, and the word was God. . . . All things were made by him" (Jn. 3:1-3). Any reading of the next 30 verses of John's account of the Gospel makes clear that John was speaking of Jesus of Nazareth.

Not only did John make such a claim, Jesus made an even stronger claim of himself. He told some astonished listeners, "Before Abraham was, I am." He was claiming divinity and his listeners knew it. His listeners understood so clearly that they treated him as a blasphemer, wanting to stone Him to death (Jn. 8:56-59). The Greek verb used for "I am" is a verb of infinite past-present-future time-linear dimension. It says, "I always was, I now am, and I shall always be." Here, Jesus identified himself as eternally co-existent with His Father, Jehovah. We get this transliterated name (Jehovah) from the Hebrew name for God, "YHWH." (The Hebrews wrote no vowels.) He identified Himself with YHWH (Jehovah). Either Jesus is who He said He is, or He was a mentally ill egomaniac, or worse—the greatest charlatan in the history of the world. That conclusion is left to each individual.

Although linguistic scholars have struggled to understand the meaning of God's name, Jehovah (YHWH), the generally accepted meaning may be stated as, "I am who I have always been and who I shall always be." Jesus identified Himself with this Eternal One—the Eternal I AM.

By the time God spoke His enfleshed Word, Jesus Christ, into the world, the human race was still so limited in its view of God, those to whom He came were barely able to hear or see such a complete revelation. Only a small number could grasp the truth. Jesus met with a near-total resistance. Even after Jesus' death and resurrection, God is seen as continuing His revelation of Himself. For instance, if we look into the history of God's early encounter with the Jewish race, we see that He wanted them to make a major effort to lead the pagans to worship Him (Genesis 12:3). But with their limited prior knowledge (or understanting) of God, their minds—their spirit could not believe it. No! Jehovah was *their* God. The *Jews* alone were His chosen people—they and they alone.

SOME MODERN HERESIES

The Jews of that day had formed their theological image of God as if it had been carved in stone. Many leaders of modern churches continue to promote much of the Old Testament image of God as if God's Old Testament image had been carved in stone—as if God had never revealed His true nature in the person of Jesus, God's fullest revelation of Himself to humankind.

Perhaps I should illustrate the heresy that promotes an early Old Testament perception of the nature of God.

1) After my friend's son was killed in an automobile accident, a member of the clergy assured her that "God does not put more on us than we can bear." After my wife was diagnosed with small cell carcinoma in a lung that had spread to her liver, bones, and brain, I, too was supposed to feel comforted by those same words spoken by a gospel minister. Did that minister really expect me to find some gospel (good news) in the suggestion that God had put those cancerous tumors in my wife? Having read the four accounts of the life of my Lord in the New Testament many times, I have found nothing to support such an accusation against God. Indeed, instead of giving people various diseases, I read of Jesus, God's fullest revelation of Himself, promoting the cure of people's diseases!

The nearest passage of scripture I can find that someone may have misconstrued as relating to "God not putting more on us than we can bear" is I Corinthinans 10:13. "There hath no temptation taken you but such as is common to man: but God is faithful, who will not suffer you to be tempted above that ye are able; but will with the temptation also make a way to escape, that ye may be able to bear it." The passage is talking about temptation—not about sickness, death of loved ones, or accidents! In that passage, Paul was assuring us that when we are tempted, God offers us a way to escape without acting on the temptation.

2) A speeding, drunken driver lost control of his car while turning a street corner and instantly killed two little first-grade girls. Pulpiteers were quoted as having said that God must have caused it as His way of trying to tell their parents something. For weeks, their parishioners echoed the accusation. They

were essentially accusing God of using a drunken driver to kill those two small children. They were blaming God for doing something the law of the land puts people in prison for doing. **No one can point to anything in the life of Jesus that would suggest that He would kill children to teach their parents something!** Instead, he was kind to them.

3) A lineman, working on high voltage wires atop a utility pole made a mistake and was electrocuted. The pastor told the widow and three children that he doesn't understand why things like that happen, but "God doesn't make mistakes" and to remember that "God is in control." When we do not know what to say, it usually is better to say nothing. I wish I knew how many thousands of times I heard those sort of comments in the room of my patients who were sick and threatened by death.

And many wonder why so many people abandon the church within six months after a death in the family. They are angry at God! After having served as a professional hospital chaplain for thirty-one years, I wrote a whole book on anger against God: *God in the Hands of Angry Sinners.*[13] If a co-worker had killed her husband and the father of her three children, the whole family would have been angry with the murderer. Why would she and the children *not* have been angry with a god she believes to have murdered by electrocution that husband and father atop a utility pole?

Within the context of such a tragedy almost everyone hears "God doesn't make mistakes" as an accusation against God. It is a not so subtle a way of saying, "God caused this tragedy, but it is a mistake only in our eyes. Don't hold it against God because God doesn't ever make mistakes." Where in all of the New Testament do we get the image of God as One who sickens, mames, or kills?

Have we arrived at a clue to such ignorant accusations against God? Deep in the psyche of many modern North Americans is the Old Testament image of a God who ultimately kills everybody! A very high percent of our population believes that God is the Grand Killer of humanity! Having listened at the bedside of my patients and their families for thirty-one years, I am forced to this belief!

And within the context of pain or sorrow we are likely to be told, "You hurt, but remember that God is in control." My first wife lived in perpetual pain for the last twelve years of her life. We had been married for 54 years when she developed cancer and died seven weeks and two days after the diagnosis. Roughly two years later, I remarried. When my lovely, precious wife of only four months died seven weeks and six days after having been diagnosed with cancer, was I supposed to feel comforted by being reassured that "God is in control?" What do people (Christians?) mean by it? I have repeatedly read the entire Bible. I majored in studies of the Christian religion at a highly respected Christian university. I majored in theology at one of the nation's finest theological seminaries. I studied three years in an internship and residency programs to prepare me to minister to my patients as a hospital chaplain. I have earned two doctoral degrees from Christian institutions of higher education, but no one has yet adequately explained what they mean when they tell me, "God is in control." With those words, I hear people telling me that God caused all of my first wife's suffering from arthritis and that He finally killed them both with cancer. In my mind, such an accusation against my Lord is nothing short of blasphemy. Perhaps I am wrong, but if I do not understand with my educational background, what is the typical frustrated soul in the pew of a church expected to understand? In seventy-eight years, I have heard my share of "double talk," and those who have tried to explain have only spoken gibberish.

At least as early as the Biblical story of Job, men were living with that which Biblical theologians call the Deuteronomic Formula. In essence, those who adhere to the Deuteronomic Formula believe that God gives good people health and wealth, but to evil people, God gives sickness and poverty. The entire book of Job deals with the Deuteronomic Formula that is *as alive early in the twenty-first century as it was 4,000 years ago* in the days of Job.

The book of Job refutes that belief in its opening chapter. God declared that Job was an upright man who revered God and avoided evil (cf. Job 1:8). However, Job suffered great losses of family, wealth, and health, and God is viewed throughout much of the Old Testament as bringing destruction into human life.

The people believed that everything that happened was by the deliberate, active hand of God. Today, when millions of us hear that God is in control, we hear that God causes all accidents—that He induces arthritis into backs, knees and hip joints—that God inserts bacteria into babies' spines to cause meningitis—that God "knew best" when He injected small cell carcinoma into my wife's lungs that spread like wildfire into her bones, liver, and brain. Nonsense! Blasphemy! My first wife agonized with rheumatoid and osteo arthritis that she inherited from her father. My second died from small cell carcinoma because she lived daily in the presence of second-hand smoke for more than fifty years!

Jesus clearly rejected the belief that the hand of God is always active in the creation human tragedy. On an occasion when men were assuming that God brought all tragedies into people's lives, Jesus asked, When ". . .*those eighteen, upon whom the **tower** in Siloam fell, and slew them, think ye that they were sinners above all men that dwelt in Jerusalem?*" (Lk. 13:4)

Much of the church continues to live with an Old Testament understanding of the nature of God.[14] Much of the world is saying, "Tell me about the nature of your god and then I will tell you if I believe in Him. How can I worship a god who does things for which we imprison or execute men? If you will tell me of the God who reveals Himself in Jesus as He is characterized in the New Testament, I am ready to worship Him."

I keep remembering a seminary professor who was highly criticized after he said that he believed that modern preaching drove away from the church as many as it attracted into it.

Has God changed, or has human understanding of Him changed?

PROGRESSIVE REVELATION OR PROGRESSIVE UNDERSTANDING

God had slowly revealed Himself more and more fully for thousands of years. Unfortunately, many Christians become distressed at the very idea of God having progressively revealed Himself to the human race, or that *man's capacity for understanding* God progressed across the ages of Biblical history. They are afraid that the concept attacks the Bible, or their concept of Biblical inspiration. Or they are afraid that it attacks their belief that God is "the same yesterday, and today, and forever." Not at all! God has not changed! It is in the Bible that we see God progressively making His true nature known. (Where else could we find it?) The concept of progression in humankind's understanding of God may be viewed in one of two approaches.

As we study the Biblical accounts, we cannot clearly determine whether we are seeing a progression in God's revelation of Himself, or if instead, we are seeing humankind's "progressive understanding" of the nature of God. We will approach the subject as if they were the same.

The concept of progressive revelation holds that each writer of the Bible received a true revelation from God, and the writer understood that revelation within the limitations imposed by his previous experience, his culture, his custom, and his geographical-historical setting. God's Holy Spirit inspired the writer to write his understanding of that which had been revealed to him. As humankind was either able to understand more about God, or God revealed more of Himself, the Bible clearly shows a growing understanding of God's nature.

ABRAHAM'S IMAGE OF GOD COMPARED TO MOSES'

To make the point, and for the sake of brevity, we will begin with "Father Abraham." From out of Mesopotamia, the land between the Tigris and the Euphrates Rivers, from among people who worshiped the heavenly bodies, God called Abram. As Abram obeyed God by traveling into Canaan and on into Egypt, he became acquainted with men who worshiped hundreds of different gods created by the hands and minds of the various peoples. However, to Abram, whom God renamed Abraham, God had revealed Himself as the one and only, living, thinking, all-powerful God who sought a covenant interpersonal relationship with Abraham and his descendants. In Abraham's limited understanding of the nature of God, Abraham shows no compunction about giving his wife for the Egyptian ruler's sexual gratification. Neither does Abraham show misgivings in taking Hagar for a surrogate wife and mother of his child. God shows no disapproval of his actions. In the Ten Commandments, God revealed to Moses that He forbade such behavior.

Four hundred years pass, and the children of Israel are enslaved in Egypt. God commissions Moses to lead his people out of Egypt into Canaan. Moses approaches the Pharaoh demanding freedom for the slaves. God wants freedom for His people, and through Moses, God promises the Pharaoh that catastrophes will fall upon the Pharaoh and his people if he refuses to let the enslaved Israelites go free.

God is then depicted as removing all of the Pharaoh's decision-making capacity. We are told that God repeatedly "hardened Pharaoh's heart" (Ex 10:20, 27; 11:10; 14:8) keeping him from doing as God commands. The Pharaoh and his people are doomed. God makes a command. However, God keeps the Pharaoh from fulfilling the command. Then, because he has repeatedly failed to fulfill the command, he and his people are repeatedly punished! Finally, the Pharaoh permits the Israelites to go free. But while the Israelites are crossing the Red Sea on dry ground, God again "hardened Pharaoh's heart" and causes him and his army to follow the Israelites into the waters where God causes them to drown (Ex. 14:8-9). Such inconsistent behavior on the part of God seems to have created no moral/ethical/spiritual problem for the mind of the early Hebrews. The ancient writer never approaches the issue of Pharaoh's having been forced to sin by his disobedience to God. Nor does the Biblical writer respond to God's apparent unfair behavior by making a demand, forbidding the fulfillment of the demand, and then punishing Pharaoh and his people for not fulfilling the demand.

A short time later, in approximately 1462 B. C., God gave to Moses the Ten Commandments. Only four related directly to the people's relationship with Him. The remaining six related to people's relationship with one another. God soon revealed more requirements for "His chosen people." Man's understanding of God had suddenly turned a corner. Never before in human history had a god cared about how human beings treated one another. A God who cared enough for human beings to demand compassion for widows and orphans, and condemned extortion or usury must have seemed truly strange to the inhabitants of the land into which they eventually moved.

However, even in the Ten Commandments, at times, God seems to be speaking only to men. Anthropologist, William J. Fielding notes, "In the Tenth Commandment the woman is mentioned together with the domestic servants and domestic animals. The man is warned not to covet his neighbor's wife, nor his man-servant, nor his maid-servant, nor his ox, nor his ass, nor anything that is his neighbor's. Woman, then, is treated rather as an impersonal object, a piece of property, that man should not covet if someone else's possession" (Fielding, p. 100). Throughout the Old Testament, women generally are viewed as man's possession.

However, by the time God reveals Himself in the person of Jesus, we see Him as compassionate, loving, caring, and forgiving. To the "woman at the well" He offered the "water of life." To the "woman caught in adultery" He offered forgiveness. To the woman who washed his feet with tears, he offered compassion. In behalf of the woman who anointed his head with expensive ointment, He demanded patience. To the woman who "touched the hem of His garment" he gave healing. Women who came to know Him personally, loved Him. Although not members of the "inner circle" of the twelve apostles, they were among his closest followers. He respected them and they knew it.

By the time God gave His Law to Moses, for more than a thousand years, the commonly understood law of retaliation had dominated the minds of the people of the entire Mediterranean region. The law of retaliation had demanded the taking of an "eye for an eye and a tooth for a tooth, hand for a hand, a foot for a foot , and life for a life."

We can only wonder how the history of the world would have flowed differently if the people had heard the Mosaic Law as demanding the *giving* of one's eye to someone whose eye had been taken by intent or by careless accident. Across the centuries, in that region of the world, men have retaliated deed for deed in an unending tit-for-tat. Human beings have never been able to live in community with others without feeling themselves occasionally violated by a neighbor. One never has to look far to see evidence that one has been treated unjustly.

What would have happened differently in the flow of world events if the law of retaliation instead had been understood as giving an eye for an eye, a tooth for a tooth etc.? What would have happened if every individual had obeyed that teaching by saying, in effect, "Oh, how terrible of me. I have destroyed your eye, and I have knocked out your tooth. In a moment of anger, I wronged you. My words, 'I'm sorry,' must sound empty to you. I can offer no monetary compensation. Here, I stand before you giving you my eye and my tooth for you to destroy. Whatever 'payment' you extract, I will not return in any way. Let's let this issue end right here." Might that have been the intent of the law as recorded in Ex. 21:23-25—give life for life, eye for eye, tooth for tooth," etc.?

Knowing humankind as He did, it is difficult to believe that God did not know that retaliation would beget retaliation that would beget retaliation, in an unending cycle. It seems entirely possible that the hearers of the law as given in Exodus 21:23-25 simply did not have ears to hear the intent of God's instruction. Since more than a thousand years of cultural influence had demanded the *taking* of an "eye for an eye and a tooth for a tooth," it seems highly probable that the recipients of those instructions believed God was blessing that which they were already accustomed to doing.

Let's "flash forward" in time and hear Jesus as He unveils the nature of God more fully. "Ye have heard that it hath been said, An eye for an eye, and a tooth for a tooth: But I say unto you, That ye resist not evil: but whosoever shall smite thee on thy right cheek, turn to him the other also" (Matthew 5:38-39). Who, better than Jesus, was more able to add to humankind's understanding of the nature of God?

Moses' Image of God Compared to Jeremiah's

In years that followed Moses, men believed that God punished entire nations for the sins of one man (Joshua 7).

However, by the time of Jeremiah, God made it clear through His prophet that from that time forth, "they shall *no more* say that their fathers have eaten sour grapes and their children's teeth have been set on edge. *But everyone shall die for his own iniquity*" (Emphasis added--Jeremiah 31:29-30). God had not changed His mind. Ever so slowly, Hebrew understanding of God's nature was progressing. (What serious minded person of today is not trying to understand better the nature of Jehovah, the God and father of Jesus Christ?)

Moses' Image of God Compared to Later Prophets'

Moses had clearly understood that God demanded animal sacrifices even though he nor others understood the reason. By the time of the prophets Isaiah, Micah, Amos, and Hosea, they understood that God's judgment was upon empty religion that neglected justice, mercy, and righteousness. During a time in which the people were sacrificing animals daily in the temple, Hosea wrote for God, ". . . I desired mercy, and not sacrifice; and the knowledge of God more than burnt offerings" (Hosea 6:6).

23

JONAH'S IMAGE OF GOD COMPARED TO JESUS'

Furthermore, from this general period of history, we read of Jonah. The people of this period were certain that God resided in the Holy of Holies of the temple in Jerusalem. He cursed and blessed the people of that geographic region and His punishment could reach out within hundreds of miles. However, to get away from God, Jonah was certain that he could flee "from the presence of the Lord" by going to a far away land (probably the land we know as Spain, cf. Jonah 1:3). Jonah's perception of God as a regional deity is far different from the perception of God revealed by Jesus who spoke of being with his people always (cf. Matthew 28:20). He further reassured that the Holy Spirit would forever be with His people (cf. John 14:16).

Following Jonah and seven hundred more years in human history, God seems to have said, "Those human beings still do not adequately understand My nature and almost from their beginning, they also have needed a means of redemption." The time was right. ". . . when the fullness of time was come, God sent forth his Son, made of woman, made under the law, to redeem them that were under the law, that we might receive the adoption of sons" (Gal. 4:4). When we read the four accounts of the Gospel, we see Jehovah's fullest revelation of Himself as manifest in the life and person of Jesus the Christ—the Messiah—the King of God's Kingdom here on earth.

JESUS, THE PERFECT, COMPLETE IMAGE OF GOD

Church leaders, for at least the past half century, have been talking about the need for revival within the church. Can we truly expect a revival in Christ's Church without revising the church's message to affirm loudly and clearly that Jesus truly is the Messiah (King) who demands habitual obedience of the citizens of His Kingdom?

SIN 2
FAILURE TO OBEY
JESUS' LAW OF LOVE:
A NEW COMMANDMENT

I give unto you,
That ye love one another;
as I have loved you, that ye
also love one another. (Jn. 13:34)

For more than fourteen centuries, the Jews had lived with the Ten Commandments that God had given through Moses on Mount Sinai. Then, Jesus startled his followers with the statement, "I'm giving you a new commandment." "Love one another as I have loved you" became that which many have called the eleventh commandment (John 13:34). The God of Heaven and Earth, who had given the original Ten Commandments, was issuing fresh instructions—even with the strength of a commandment through the mouth of His Son, the King of Heaven and Earth. Jesus did not say this was something He would *like* for His followers to do. He did not say this was something they ought or should do. The Messiah—Christ—the King of the Kingdom of God was issuing a royal edict to His subjects—to those who consented to his government: LOVE ONE ANOTHER.

What did Jesus mean?

We cannot know that unless we understand the meaning of the word that Jesus used for love. Love has so many different meanings and is so overly used that almost no one knows what it means.

On dozens of occasions, from a public platform I have asked my listeners to give me a working definition of the word "love." Most have sat in awkward silence with quizzical expressions. Those few brave souls who ventured an answer sounded somewhat like college sophomore philosophers. On far more occasions, in my role as a professional Marriage and Family Therapist[15] I have asked my counselees to give a good working definition of the word, "love." With few exceptions, my counselees have vaguely defined love as some sort of warm feeling.

When I have asked couples who have come to me for pre-marital counseling what they mean when they say, "I love you," their responses generally can be described in a few representative answers similar to those given by others. "I like how she makes me feel." "I feel some kind of warm feeling for him." "I like being with her." "I care for him."

Are they wrong answers? Are they inappropriate answers? Of course not. But when the answers stop there, the answers are woefully incomplete. The kind of love they describe is not the kind of love that keeps a man and woman enjoying their relationship until death do they part. And it certainly is not the kind of love about which Jesus spoke when He decreed, "Love one another; as I have loved you, also love one another" (cf. John 13:34). The phrase, "as I have loved you" is the key to our understanting the meaning of the kind of love about which Jesus was talking. His lifestyle was the pattern! He consistently, habitually worked in the best interests of everyone he encountered. Not only was He telling them (and us) to love, He was demonstrating how to do it.

The American public does not understand the most important meaning of the word "love." And with few exceptions, the church has no better understanding of the love about which Jesus spoke than the general public. Also, as I have been listening for many years to the spokesmen in the pulpits of the churches of America, I have concluded that a large percentage of the clergy has no better understanding of love than their parishioners. Are our seminaries failing their students? Are our theological seminaries teaching their students the practical, day in and day out meaning of the word love, as Jesus repeatedly used it? Recognizing some exceptions, the "better educated" clergy seems no more knowledgeable about the meaning of love than the man in the remote mountain pulpit who failed to graduate from high school.

Of course, you can find exceptions, but the statement generally appears true. Therefore, the church has accepted the world's definition of love as some sort of good feeling. *Instead of defining love to the world and then demonstrating love to the surrounding world, the church appears to have permitted the surrounding world to define the meaning of love to it.* The love of which Jesus spoke can never be defined by some kind of pleasant feeling. Feelings can shift as quickly as the wind. If I limit love to a good feeling, my love for my wife disappears with a bad bowl of chili.

During the late 1940s, the church loudly and repeatedly proclaimed, "The family that prays together stays together." We believed it! We believed that a couple who attends public worship together is going to build a more enjoyable and lasting bond in their relationship than the flimsy bond in the relationships of others. We believed that the couple who worshiped together was being taught a higher standard of moral-ethical behavior than the rest of the world. We were being taught to love! But who was teaching the meaning of the word love as Jesus it? Who was teaching the church how to love? "What" without "how" often amounts to nothing!

Then, a few years ago, some of us were startled to learn that the divorce rate was as high among couples in churches across the United States as it was among the general population. "What? That can't be correct! The church has been teaching people to love one another," we said.

Then we learned that the statement really was incorrect. The divorce rate among members of the modern North American church is actually higher than it is among the general population. George Barna, president and founder of Barna Research Group, a Christian-based body, has done much research on the subject. He has commented: "While it may be alarming to discover that born again Christians are more likely than others to experience a divorce, that pattern has been in place for quite some time. Even more disturbing, perhaps, is that when those individuals experience a divorce many of them feel their community of faith provides rejection rather than support and healing. But the research also raises questions regarding the effectiveness of how churches minister to families. The ultimate responsibility for a marriage belongs to the husband and wife, but the high incidence of divorce within the Christian community challenges the idea that churches provide truly practical and life-changing support for marriages."

When the Dallas Morning News, a Dallas, TX newspaper reported this information many readers were angered. George Barna replied that he stands by his data, even though it is upsetting. He said, "We rarely find substantial differences between the moral behavior of Christians and non-Christians." Perhaps even more disturbing to many Christians is a report that the Bible Belt has the highest divorce rate in the US. How can this be true? Someone intelligently responded, "Why would the divorce rate be lower in the church when the church generally holds the same definition of love as the rest of the world?" We of the church have accepted the general definition of love as defined by the society instead of defining love to the society! We have simply said, "Love one another," without defining the word for love that Christ used.

The New Testament definition for love is far different from that of the American culture where millions who claim the Christian faith live out their lives. Christians serve a King (Christ) under whose law we are commanded to conduct ourselves. The Savior-King even said this commandment was second only to the commandment to love God (Matthew 22:39). If the commandment to love others is second to the commandment to love God, is it possible that He considers the failure to love others as the second most important and destructive sin! The modern church cannot afford to continue living in the sin of disobedience to Christ's law of love, whether by ignorance, neglect, or rebellious decision. **If the church does not teach the meaning of love as Jesus used it, who will?**

The basic problem with understanding and living by the law of love grows out of a limitation in the development of the English language. It is a problem of English speaking people around the world. When we English speaking people speak of love we have only one word to use. Consequently, we say that we love our mate, we love our child, we love our parents, we love our brothers and sisters, we love our dog, we love apples, and we may even say that we love God.

However, we do not mean the same thing each time we use the word. We may recognize that we mean something different when we speak of the love for a parent as compared to love for a sister. We know there's a difference between the love for our spouse and the love for our child. And we know that we are not speaking of the same thing when we speak of loving our mother and when we speak of loving an intimate friend. We know there are differences in the love we have for various people, but we may not be able to describe or define those differences. The differences are great and they are important.

Our forefathers, while in the long process of creating our language, simply did not create words to differentiate among the various forms of love. Those who forged the Greek language were either more fortunate or wiser than those who fashioned the English language. The Greeks coined several different words to use when speaking of different forms of love. When a Greek spoke of love, he could choose the word that would say precisely what he meant. When writers of the New Testament wanted to tell what Jesus had said about love, they wrote in the Greek language. However, when scholars wish to translate any document from Greek into English, they might have any of four basic Greek words before them, but only one English word to use for translating our Scriptures. Therefore, we end up with one word—"love" which holds several very different meanings.

To better understand Jesus' commandment to love one another, we need to look at the four most commonly used Greek words for love that have been translated into the English language.

When the Greeks wished to speak of their warm, tender, affectionate love for family or friend, they could choose from various forms of the words *phileo* (from which Philadelphia, the city of brotherly love, gets its name) or *storge* which was usually reserved for the child-parent relationships.

STORGE

The *storge* form of love may be described as an over-under relationship with one in authority over the other and one dependent upon the other—as a child is dependent on the parent and the parent must be in protective leadership authority over the child. Feelings of affection and endearment are common.

This is the only form of love that results in the separation of the participants. One of the greatest responsibilities we have as parents is to help our children develop their sense of independence to the level that one day they can say, "Thank you for all that you have provided through the years. I love you. Give me your blessing and rejoice with me as I go out into the world to build my life. I'll stay in touch occasionally. Bye."

PHILEO

The other family-related Greek root word for love that I mentioned a few paragraphs back was the word *phileo*. This is the form of love we see in a healthy relationship between a brother and sister, between brothers, or sisters, or between intimate friends. Your spouse should be your most cherished friend. This form of love also is characterized by feelings of affection.

In our culture, with only one word to speak of love, most men are afraid to tell the dearest male friend that he loves him fearing that he will be misunderstood. He fears that he might be heard as speaking homosexually. Combat veterans who feel they have been to Hell and back together are likely to form bonds of friendship that last a lifetime. The bond of deep friendship shared between any two people is included in the form of love about which we are thinking. However, even those combat veterans with feelings of affection for their friends may never say, "I love you." They fear that someone will think they speak of eros, an entirely different form of love.

EROS

The Greeks used forms of the word *eros* (from which we get our word "erotic") to speak of love that was possessive, or self-gratifying. It is love motivated by the hope or expectation of personal gain.

This word was used in reference to sexual desire or to the sex act.

Because of the meaning of this word, it is correct to say that a couple, "made love" last night. Of course, this love also is loaded with feelings. We do not even wait until our teen years to experience these feelings. Those who assume that love is only a feeling, tend also to assume that sexual interest is the basis of a lasting relationship without commitment. "Shacking up" has gained respect under the heading of "living together" and has given rise to the term "significant other" in reference to the person with whom one is cohabiting. In the U.S., during the period in which adults were unmarried, one in three has lived with someone of the opposite sex. Thirty-seven percent of them profess the Christian faith.

Neither *storge* nor *eros* are found in texts of the New Testament.

AGAPÉ

Note that in each of the forms of love described in the foregoing paragraphs, feelings were an important factor. When Jesus declared the Eleventh Commandment, he ordered us to love with a form of love that is virtually unrelated to any feeling. Jesus chose to command us to follow the way of life that lives out the richest, most beneficial, most profound form of love known in Heaven or on earth. He chose *agapé*. This form of love is characterized, not by feelings, but by behavior. For want of this form of love, one may say, "You say you love me, but you don't show it."

Various forms of the word *agapé* denote a self-giving love to one who does not necessarily merit that love. This form of love *wants and works for the other person's highest good*—even the highest good of an enemy (Matthew 5:44). This form of love seeks to give without motive to receive. It defines no conditions to be met by the other person before the love is given. It simply asks, "How can I act in the other person's behalf or best interests?" This form of love acts, not on the basis of warm feeling. It acts on the basis of a decision to act in keeping with that which we recognize to be for the other person's good.

Since the agapé form of love is primarily a way of treating the other person, it is often highly visible. (If, without your knowledge, I were to drop into your home as an invisible guest, what would I see that would convince me that you love your mate? What would I see during the course of a day or over a period of a week that would convince me? What would I see in your lifestyle that would tell me that you are consistently working in your mate's best interests?)

I really am saying that love in its highest form is a way of behaving—of acting—of treating that other person. Since this form of love is a verb, it requires representative action. This is how Jesus could issue the command to love.

He did not use a form of the word *phileo*. He was not instructing us to conjure up some kind of "warm fuzzy" feelings for others—even for our enemies. He certainly did not use a form of the word *eros*. He was not suggesting the arousal of prurient interests in others, although a homosexual group once revealed their ignorance by suggesting that Jesus was homosexual because the New Testament speaks of a "disciple whom Jesus loved" (John 21:7). The writer did not use a form of the word *eros*, he used a form of the word *agapé*. This was a disciple for whom Jesus had a special concern that called for special attention.

All of this shocks many people. Our culture has so limited the meaning of the word love that we have a hard time conceiving of a form of love without some sort of warm indefinable feeling. When I have discussed this with couples in the marriage counseling office, I have seen wide-eyed surprise on many occasions.

When love is limited to some kind of feeling, if I say, "I love you," you are left to your imagination. Or you may think, "I know how I feel when I say those words. Therefore, you must mean the same thing." If I only tell you that I love you, you don't even know if I mean it. But if you recognize that love is a way of acting (behaving) you can watch how I treat you and know if I love you. Love, as it is revealed in the person of Jesus Christ says, "I want what is best for you. I'm working in your best interests, and I want you to be working in the best interests of others also."

Something was wrong (missing) during my developmental years. I did not learn the meaning of the word "Love" as Jesus used it from my pastors, my college, seminary, and graduate school professors, the radio and television preachers I heard, or from my supervisors in three and a half years of internship and residency for training to serve as a hospital chaplain. I had to learn it by linguistic studies in *books*! I am simply one example of the millions who are being failed by our Christian educational system. The world is eager and thrilled to hear the meaning of the *agapé* form of love.

A young woman once wrote to me a letter several weeks after I had discussed the meaning of love with a group of high school students. She said that my explanation of the meaning of love had been the "talk of the campus" for days after my lecture. She went on to say that her boy friend had been pressuring her for a sex relationship. After our discussion she told him, "You say that if I truly loved you, I would have sex with you. But if you truly love me, you want what is best for me. Having a sex relationship outside of marriage would not be in either of our best interests over the long run. Therefore, if you really love me, you won't pressure me for sex."

The word "*agapé*" that I keep using, is the word Jesus used most often when referring to love. The New Testament denies no feeling of love, but it adds a dimension that makes love so concrete that it is even subject to direct orders (from the Supreme Commander). "I'm giving you a new commandment. Love (*agapé*) one another." (John 13:34).

Jesus chose a form of the word that made it into a continuous action verb. The essence of His command required, "Do this (love) as an ongoing and continuing practice!" This is the form of love necessary for an enjoyable, lasting love relationship between a man and a woman. Without it, the quality of the relationship quickly deteriorates. It also is the form of love necessary for all who surrender to the Lordship of Christ as citizens of the Kingdom of God.

31

We don't wait for the right mood to put this form of love into action. We act in the other person's behalf simply because we observe their need, and the *agapé* form of love requires that we act on our recognition of the need.

Even if Jesus had not given the commandment to practice the *agapé* form of love, I still would have to say these things based on my many years of listening in the marriage counseling office.

Though much of the English language has been derived from the Greek language, we could have profited from them even more if we had borrowed more on their different words to express love.

The healthy love between husband and wife must combine the *"phileo"* (friendship), *"eros"* (sexual), and *"agapé"* (behavioral), forms of love into their marriage.

A former generation often used the expression, "Charity begins at home." That word "charity," was used in 1611 by the translators of the King James Bible.[16] The love Jesus commanded, the law of love, begins with our family and reaches out to all who are a part of the context in which we live. It is a part of the faith decision to trust God enough to do as he commands through His son Jesus.

For one who is married, the highest expression of love for the mate says in effect, "I want that which is best for you, and I am committed to work hard toward that which is in your best interest for as long as I live." Deep relationships develop from the practice of love working actively in that other person's best interests.

When each person is seeking and working in behalf of the other's best interests, neither is short-changed. Both are enriched. While each is giving in abundance, each is receiving in abundance.

While love is supposed to be the ideal motive for marriage, rarely is the ideal achieved—largely because most people insist on defining love only as a feeling. Paul wrote, "Do not be conformed to this world, but be transformed by the renewing of your mind, that you may prove what is good and acceptable and perfect will of God" (Romans 12:2).

When husbands and wives of the church begin treating one another with this form of love which Jesus commanded, the eyes of the world will watch in amazement. The world will see divorce virtually eliminated from among its members.

Or will it?

Another issue exists that probably always will exaggerate the church's divorce statistics. It has revealed itself behind the closed doors of the marriage counselor's office, and it has revealed itself to pastors who listen carefully to their parishioners.

In the midst of disaster, people quite often try to bargain with God. A dying man may promise to be a better husband, or that he will begin to give a tithe of his income to the church if God will heal him.

In a similar mode, many couples turn to God when their marriage is in danger of dying. Too many times, I have heard words that said in effect, "My marriage is in trouble. If I believe strong enough and pray hard enough, God will make our marriage right." During forty-five years of marriage counseling, I have never seen God make a relationship right when one of both the husband and wife continued in patterns of behavior that are destructive to the relationship.

In a similar vain, many couples recognize that their marriage is in trouble and decide to "give God a try." They begin attending worship services of the local church and become members. They may even "make professions of faith." But without repentance and submission to the re-creative work of God in their lives, nothing changes. Without behavior improvement, their relationship does not improve! Invariably, bad marital relationships grow out of some kind of destructive behavior. Bad feelings grow out of bad behavior. And bad relationships continue to be bad when destructive behavior continues. Perhaps once a year a marriage counselor hears someone say, "Help! I've messed up our marriage." The other couples always are certain that the real problem is created by the spouse. They convince themselves that the trouble in the marriage is the other person's fault. Without confession (admission of error) there is no repentance (turn from destructive to constructive behavior), and without repentance, there is no improvement in the relationship.

About as many people find it difficult to apply that truth to marriage relationships as they do in applying the same truth to their relationship with God. After a few months, the couple may feel that God has failed them, or that the church did not help. Those couples who have made a shallow decision to "give God a try" without a life-transforming faith in Him, later end their marriage in divorce. That means that another "family of the church" is added to the table of "church and divorce" statistics.

All too often, they are right. All too often the church has not helped. We have simply told them to love. Accepting the world's definition of the word love, we have left people to understand love as a feeling. We have not told them HOW to love and then criticized them for failing to do so. Then, when their marriage relationship ends in divorce, we have failed to support those whose souls that are bleeding, or we have openly rejected them.

Several years ago, I walked through an open door leading into the chapel of our hospital. Out of the corner of my eye, through the crack at the hinges, I thought I saw someone hiding. I stopped and could hear someone crying. I slowly pulled the door back and found a young office worker sobbing. I apologized for intruding into her pain and commented that something bad obviously had happened. Would she like to step around the corner to my office where she could talk in private? In my office, still sobbing, she told me that her husband had just called and told her that he had found someone else he loved, and that he was filing for divorce that day. The word "crushed" does not adequately express her sense of devastation.

They divorced and she changed jobs. I ran into her a year later, and as she outlined the events in her life since I had seen her she told me she had left her church. I was surprised and asked "Why?" Tears filled her eyes as she told me that she had been stripped of the Sunday School class she had been teaching for several years and was told that there was no longer a place in the church for her. I wish I could say that her case is unique, but I still remember the sixteen year old girl who was told that she was no longer welcome in her church because she had given birth to a child without the benefits of marriage. I knew the girl. She was already feeling guilty and self-condemned for her mistake. Both of these women were literally pushed out of their churches at a time they most needed the love, support, and redemptive resources that Christ intended His church to be. When the church rejects, people feel that God rejects. The Berna research group has reported that churches commonly fail to support those who experience divorce. (And many of the church fail to understand why the church is often characterized as a club of self-righteous hypocrites).

Will the thousands of churches across North America ever learn the meaning of love? Will we remain guilty of telling people what to do without teaching them *how* to do it? The responsibility for change is clearly in the hands of those of us who are members of the clergy. Who else has the responsibility and the opportunity?

While serving as a hospital chaplain, I gave hundreds of lectures to laypersons of the church, telling them things they should and should not do while ministering to the sick, the dying, and the bereaved. On numerous occasions, someone has come to me after a lecture and said, "Thank you. We've been told for years that we should visit the sick, and the dying, and folks who have lost a loved one by death. But you are the first person who has ever told me *how* to do it." Pastors and Biblical teachers of the church may "beat people over the head with the Bible" for years while demanding that they love one another, *but how can their people love one another if they have not been taught **how** to do what they are being instructed to do?*

I was a carpenter at one period of my life. I needed someone to teach me the craft. I was a salesman at one period of my life. I needed someone to teach me effective sales techniques. I was an Air Force Pilot at a period of my life. I needed someone to teach me to fly an airplane. I was a hospital chaplain a period of my life. I needed someone to teach me how to effectively minister amid crises. Until my wife became too ill to care for herself, I practiced marriage and family therapy. To serve successfully in that capacity, I needed someone to teach me how to help families live enjoyably together (how to love).

Congregants of the modern church need "nuts and bolts nitty-gritty" practical instruction on how to love—how to treat one another. If we are not teaching our couples how to love in their homes, how well are we teaching our members the way to love out in the day-to-day world? Recognizing that Jesus gave the law of love, how can the church obey the law of love if its people do not know the meaning of the word—if the members are not taught how to love?

We are told that under the law of the land, ignorance of the law is no excuse. We will hope and pray that the grace of God extends to our failures out of ignorance. Whether disobedience is intentional or unintentional, the consequences of failing to love remain the same in the daily lives of the people of the church.

Having said that the Christ/King demands love (*agapé*) behavior, let's move from theory to practice.

- Since we are entering the field of Christian Ethics, the subject of hundreds of books, we will look at only enough examples to point the mind in the right direction.
- I have said repeatedly that love wants and works for the best interests of the other person. Therefore, the obligation to the law of love requires that we do anything that benefits other people. This requires that we ask questions and work to create emotionally and spiritually healthy answers.
- How can I help?
  Since too much help often is not in the best interests of the other person, how do I balance enough help without giving too much help?
- How can I encourage?
  Can I join or lead his/her cheering section?
  Does he/she need a pat on the back?
  Do I rejoice when he/she rejoices and weep when he/she weeps?
  When can I visit a shut-in at home or in a nursing home?
- How can I make this person's load lighter?
  Can I help prepare a meal with or without help?
  Can I wash dishes?
  Can I change the baby's diaper in the middle of the night?
  Can I help wash the car?

Can I mow the lawn or rake the leaves for a sick neighbor?

Can I sit with a sick neighbor in the hospital so that the family members can shop or go home to rest?

- How can I promote this person's emotional and spiritual growth?
- How can I make this person's journey more pleasant?
- Is being right as important as being in harmony?
- Do I work harder to assure his/her rights than I do to assure my own?
- What do I need to forgive?
- What grudge must I set aside?
- Am I patient enough with him/her, or do I allow myself to become irritated at him/her too quickly?

As we answer each question, the law of love, the Eleventh Commandment, requires corresponding appropriate action.

In summery, "How can I do unto others as I would have others do unto me?" A sage of long ago said, "The Golden Rule is the sum of the law of God. All else of the Scripture is but commentary."

SIN 3
FAILURE TO CONFRONT SIN

For the wages of sin is death,
but the gift of God is eternal life
through Jesus Christ our Lord. (Rom. 6:23)

Back in the early 1970s, Dr. Karl Menninger, one of America's most respected psychiatrists, wrote a book titled, *Whatever Became of Sin?*[17] Based on the terrible facts woven into the fabric of this book, we must conclude that early in the twenty-first century, we can answer his question. Sin has gained respectability and has joined the church. Sins of omission are as deadly as sins of commission.

However, dying churches pretend that no sin is there. The word, "sin" is almost never pronounced by anyone. How often is it spoken from the pulpit? Within recent decades, it has been made into an archaic word that does not fit into the polite language of our polite society. Since it carries a note of culpability, it is no longer a "politically correct" word for anyone to use, including the clergy. (We must not offend anyone's sensitivities.) As a "black-sheep" relative may never be called by name at a family gathering, many are uncomfortably aware of sin's presence but who calls it by its name?

Sin is not condemned for being precisely what it is: violation of the law of God. It is behavior that does not bow to the rule of God in life, behavior that habitually falls short of obedience to God's law of love, and behavior that harms or reduces the quality of any human life and the world over which God gave the human race dominion.

Approximately, 1462 B.C., God had delivered the Israelites from Egyptian slavery. During their forty year pilgrimage to the "promised land" that should have taken little more than three weeks, God saw that his people were living in a lifestyle degrading and harmful to themselves and others. They were living in sin.

GOD GAVE TEN COMMANDMENTS

On a craggy mountain on the Sinai Peninsula, God gave to Moses the foundation of all constructive human behavior. He gave the Ten Commandments. Did the violation of God's Law suddenly become "sin" on that eventful day in approximately 1462 B.C.?

Much of the world has envisioned God as having seated Himself on a mountainside overlooking the world while thinking, "I'm going to have some fun at those little creatures' expense. I'm going to give them some laws. If they violate them, I'm going to zap them. Since I'm highly self-centered, I'm going to order them not to take any gods but Me, or to make images of anything they might make into a god. Since my ego is rather easily wounded, I don't want them to take my name in vain. And since I suffer from an inferiority complex, I want them to tell me how great I am. I could require them do so daily, but I will require them to worship me only one day a week. I'll call it the Sabbath.

"Since they will tend to form their concept of my personality based on what they see in their earthly parents, especially their fathers, I will command them to honor their fathers and mothers. When they fail to do so, I'll have an extra excuse for slapping them around. Since those things called human beings are my property, I don't want them to kill one another so I'll command them not to murder. I created them with the passions to enjoy the sex act, but since I'm a bit sadistic, I'll tantalize them by forbidding them to participate in it with any but their spouses. And since they are quite greedy and dishonest, I'll tantalize them even more by forbidding them to steal, or even to desire another's possession. I suppose I should round out these commandments with an even number, so I'll insist that they not lie to or about one another."

It may sound silly or even bordering blasphemy when put into words, but I truly believe that most people believe that God's law was designed on something of a whim. Most seem to have concluded that God's law really doesn't need to be taken seriously. If it must be taken seriously, obedience is only to appease Him.

WHY WOULD GOD HAVE GIVEN THE LAW?

To better understand God's law and the reason He gave it let's examine some of the most obvious of the laws that can ultimately represent all of His law.

Was theft not "wrong" until the day God first declared, "Thou shalt not steal?" Did theft suddenly become "wrong" on that day when God made His will known on Mt. Sinai? Or did God recognize that something was intrinsically wrong in theft? Did He recognize that there is something about theft that harms people? *Theft already was wrong and because it was wrong, God commanded his people not to steal.* You may want to read that line again. Paul wrote, "Why then the law? It was added because of transgressions" (Galatians 3:19). People were harming themselves and one another. God did not want *any* of his people harmed.

Suppose that you and I are traveling across the country together. While you are in the shower, I spot your wallet or purse on the bed, and I take a ten-dollar bill. I think you probably will not even miss it and if you do, I would be among the last people you would suspect. You probably will assume that you lost count of the amount you had spent and will dismiss it from your mind. It's really not much money.

Who will have been harmed? Yes, I will have robbed you of a small amount of the fruit of your labor. The time and energy that you put into earning it will have been a waste of a small part of your life. Will you have been the only person who has been robbed? Will I not have robbed myself of something far more precious than the mere ten dollars?

By stealing, a small part of my character will have diminished (eroded). I will be less the man I was before I stole. I will not be the man I would have been if I had resisted the temptation to steal. Since my character has been slightly eroded, I will find it easier to steal again. Each time I steal, my character will continue to erode. My theft will have harmed at least two persons—you and me.

God gave the commandment against theft in the spirit of a parent who commands his child, "Don't play with matches!" God does not have to zap us. He knows the natural consequences of sin. He knows that "sin, when it is finished (grown to full flower) bringeth forth death" (James 1:15). Even the Prophet Ezekiel recognized that "the soul that keeps on sinning –lives in the practice of sinning shall die" (cf. Ezekiel 18:20).

Again, why did God command, "Thou shalt not bear false witness." He did so for precisely the same reason that He commanded against theft. If I tell a lie against you, and you are not harmed because no one believes it, at least one person still will have been harmed. I will have damaged myself. I will have eroded my character with my lie. I will not be quite the man I was before I lied, and I will not be the man I would have been if I had resisted the temptation to lie. My sin will have diminished me. It will have eroded me. I will be more disintegrated. I will have become more fragmented. Sin disintegrates the personality. The wages of sin really is death. Sin may or may not harm another, but it always harms the person who commits it. In the spirit of a loving, caring parent who commands a small child, "Don't play in the street," God the Father has commanded us, "Thou shalt not bear false witness."

God's desire for that which is best for the human race (*agapé*/love) is to be found in each of the Ten Commandments. Some are simply more obvious than others.

Only *four commandments instructed humankind in their relationship with Him*. Even those ultimately resulted in behavior that benefited those who trust Him enough to obey His law.

➤ "You must have no other god but me." The teachings attributed to any other god would lead God's people into less than the most constructive lifestyles. Slavery, human sacrifices and other forms of the "Might Makes Right" theology were common among the influential neighbors of Moses' people.

➤ "Make no graven images." Their neighbors had created hundreds of images before which they bowed in worship. Each one inclined its followers to degrading and harmful behaviors.

➤ "Do not take My name (Jehovah) in vain." "Familiarity breeds contempt" is an adage well known by every person with a military background. Lack of due respect would result in disobedience to Jehovah's day-by-day leadership, which would then result in behaviors destructive to themselves and/or their neighbors.

➤ "Keep the Sabbath day holy." Keep one day in seven as a day of rest and worship. The human body needs rest, and in worship you will be reminded of the majesty and holiness of the God of all creation. Humankind would also be reminded that the lifestyle God wants for his people is superior and more constructive than any other lifestyle would be.

Six commandments instructed humankind more directly in their relationships to one another. The violation of any of the six would reap the behavior's natural consequences.

➤ "Honor your father and your mother."

➤ "Don't murder."

➤ "Don't commit adultery."

➤ "Don't steal."

➤ "Don't even yearn for that which belongs to your neighbor."

➢ "Don't lie."

These ten points formed the basis of development for all other of Jehovah's Law that was to guide all people who accepted Him as their God. The Law truly was made for man—not man for the Law (cf. Mk.2:27).[18] Every law that God gave benefited those who obeyed and/or the neighbor of those who obeyed.

A Jewish leader once asked Jesus which was the greatest of the commandments. Jesus answered, "Thou shalt love the Lord thy God with all thy heart, and with all thy soul, and with all thy mind. This is the first and great commandment. And the second is like unto it, Thou shalt love thy neighbor as thyself. *On these two commandments hang **all** the law and the prophets*"(Matthew 22:35-40). (Emphasis mine) Surely the man was wise who spoke the words, "All other Biblical writings are but commentary on those two commandments." Violation of God's law is sin.

JESUS WAS NOT AFRAID OF THE WORD "SIN."

Jesus confronted those who disobeyed His Father. And He was not concerned that others might become uncomfortable by His use of the word "sin." The Gospel writers record Jesus' use of the word more than fifty times. Can anyone read the writings of the prophets, or hear the words of John the Baptist, or of Jesus and imagine them not speaking clearly against sinful attitudes and behavior?

Do not expect to hear the word "sin" from the modern pulpit. The preacher may weep over the sins of the people, but don't expect him/her speak of their sin. It is simply not the educated, sociably acceptable thing to do.

While tactfully avoiding the word "sin," the good news of forgiveness and regeneration is also avoided. What are congregations hearing? Dr. Hollis Green has described it well in his book *Why Churches Die.*

> There is a famine in the land. Not of bread but of the Word of God. Ministers preoccupy themselves with current events and sermons with social and political implications rather than concentrating on the basic principles of life as presented in the Scripture."[19] He later wrote, "Often the content of the message is non-Biblical and deals with the whims and anxieties of man but has no spiritual basis for recovery of lost faith. Often the message is watered down to eliminate the elements which might be offensive to the uncommitted congregation. Much of the preaching is secular, unauthentic and false in terms of New Testament validity. The pulpit

constantly nags the people into doing good and attempts
to motivate and attract in the social improvement of the
community."[20]

Green could have added that some who fill the pulpit as Ministers of
the Gospel can preach for a year or more without ever delivering a message
from any of the four accounts of the Gospel of Jesus Christ. How can anyone
pretend to preach the Gospel of Jesus Christ while totally avoiding the words
of Jesus Christ?

One person has said, "I have heard that the word 'Gospel' means 'good
news.' I haven't heard any good news from the pulpit of my church in at least
a year. He just changes the subject that he's fussing about from one Sunday
to the next."

Every Minister of the Gospel would serve his/her congregation well by
reviewing the last year's sermon files while asking, "What good news have I
been proclaiming?"

Some rarely preach from the New Testament. Instead, they regularly
preach from the Old Testament while overlaying some Christian thoughts
onto it. How can the church hear the good news of God's offer of redemption
and regeneration if the pulpit is silent? How can the church hear the demands
of our Lord if the demands are never proclaimed? How can the church hear
the voice of our Lord call, "Come. Follow Me," if His heralds are silent? How
can the church hear ethical-moral precepts when the church often is not even
being taught right and wrong?[21] When sin is not declared, people enter the
church and continue in sin. How shall they hear without a preacher?

When the church does not teach right and wrong who is left to teach
morality?

If a public school attempts to do so, who is first to grab a banner and a
bullhorn to rally public protest? The church! Many of the church have carried
other banners in protest of the Supreme Court rulings against permitting
the display of the Ten Commandments in our public schools. But how often
does the church speak out concerning the very issues addressed by those Ten
Commandments?

But wait. *Have the individual members of the church no responsibility?* How
can the church hear when its people fail to read God's written word, the
Bible?

Does the modern church read God's Good News as presented by Mathew,
Mark, Luke, and John? If we avoid the words of Jesus, we avoid hearing
Him speak to the sins He saw among His people. Does the modern church
read the remaining books of the New Testament? The land is different. The
political climate is different. The economics are different. But the basic issues

of right and wrong among human beings remain essentially the same today as they were two thousand years ago. The value of love (*agapé*) has not changed.

A counselee once sat in my office wondering why and how she had made such a mess of her life. She said, "I have never had a pattern to live by or anyone to teach me how to live my life, I watch television and do as I see those people on TV shows do." We do not have to wonder why our culture is increasingly decadent when we realize that much of the teaching of morality is left to the entertainment industry! Much of the entertainment industry caters to the most basic and self-destructive drives of the human race.

When the Northern Kingdom of Israel was overrun by the Assyrians, the most skilled, prosperous, and educated inhabitants, including the religious leaders, were marched away and scattered among the people of other lands, as if they were seed broadcast by the farmer's hand. The Assyrians had learned that conquered people, in time, build a revolutionary force to overthrow the conqueror. Therefore, each land that the Assyrians conquered was stripped of its most able people. Those people were redistributed among other conquered lands. Therefore, those taken away totally lost their tribal, cultural, and religious identity. No one, to this day knows what happened to the "lost tribes of Israel." They became completely amalgamated among the peoples from the Persian Gulf to Constantinople.

Only the most aged, the tillers of the soil, the cultivators of grapes and olives, and other laborers were left behind. This left the land of Israel without religious leaders.

The Assyrians re-inhabited the land of Israel with peoples from other lands that they had conquered. Of course, those people brought with them, their many gods. With time, the Israelites intermarried with the newcomers which produced a hybrid race that inhabited the land. The gods that had been brought with the newcomers were adopted by the Israelites and integrated into the worship of Jehovah, the God of the Israelites. By the time Jesus trod the land we know as Palestine, those amalgamated people with their amalgamated religion were known as Samaritans. They were no longer true Jews by blood or religion. Without spokesmen to proclaim the message of God and to denounce sin, the people became ignorant and had fallen into grave sin.

But religious leaders of America's churches have not been transported into far away lands. Yet, since the middle of the twentieth century, with acknowledged exceptions, the voices that would have been expected to denounce sin have remained silent. The pulpit seems to have fallen prey to the voices of the "moral relativists," that insist that there are no absolutes and that all concepts of "right" and "wrong" are dependent on the values held by a particular culture. With too few exceptions, those who would be expected to be most vocal against such teachings have remained silent! And the evidence tells us that many of their people perish—unrepentant in sin, seeming to believe they are saved.

HOW VOCAL IS THE CHURCH AGAINST SEX ABUSE?

Much sin is conducted in absolute contempt for the law of God with the attitude that says, "Nobody! Nobody is going to control me! Nobody is going to tell me how to live my life!" How can anyone sexually abuse a member of the family without acting in blatant contempt for the Law of love? Yet, *seventy-five percent of family sexual abuse occurs in the "religious homes" of North America.* The lost are saying, "Why 'accept Christ?' Christianity doesn't really make any difference in people's lives. Christians are simply a bunch of people who say one thing and live another when they walk out of church." Atheists are laughing at Christianity while saying that the evidence declares that they live by a higher moral-ethical standard than those who profess Christianity.

- Sexual abuse (especially of children) is a practice of the occult. Hiding behind the mask of Christianity, many are practicing Satanism! (Many serve him without ever admitting it.) When I began theological and psychological studies in the mid 1950s, estimates of sexual abuse in homes were estimated at one percent. Some spokespersons who were considered to be extremists were suggesting five percent. By the '70s we concluded that the figures were really closer to fifteen percent. By the decade of the 1990s estimates were running as high as thirty-eight percent and no one knowledgeable of the issues estimated less than fifteen percent. What do the best estimates look like in the first decade of the 2000's?
- 1 in 4 girls is sexually abused before the age of 18.
- 1 in 6 boys is sexually abused before the age of 18.
- An estimated 39 million survivors of childhood sexual abuse exist in America today.

Similar to what we know of the last half or the twentieth century, even within the walls of their own homes, children are at risk for sexual abuse.

- 30-40% of victims are abused by a family member.
- 75% of family sexual abuse occurs in the "religious homes" of North America.
- Another 50% are abused by someone outside of the family whom they know and trust.
- Approximately, 40% are abused by older or larger children whom they know.
- Therefore, only 10% are abused by strangers.

I have dealt with so many people who have been sexually abused that I sometimes wondered if my name had been placed on someone's referral list for such issues. However, when I inquired, I found that most were coming to me without knowing of my extensive experience work with the sexually abused.

I will not counsel the abuser. To do so, I too would have had to spend months—perhaps years in therapy. I built up too much rage against abusers during the forty-five years I served as a therapist. I would need someone to help me deal with my own anger.

Every hog farmer in the country and I know how to stop repeat offenders of sexual crimes, but legal authorities keep saying that castration would be "cruel and unusual punishment." I keep hearing that it would be unconstitutional. Neutering would not be nearly as cruel as what sexual abusers do to their victims!)

I will not debate the accuracy or inaccuracy of the researchers who report that seventy-five percent of all sexual abuse in America occurs in "religious families." I am not in a position to know—nor do not know the statisticians' definition of a "religious family." But I am in a position to know that the sexual abuse is high in the church and anyone who has watched the television news stories unfold knows that even church leaders are often involved in the most damaging scandalous sexual misconduct. Early in the second millennium, one of the world's largest Christian bodies has not even been able to get a "zero tolerance" policy established by their worldwide leader. Even one abuse of one person by another to accommodate the sexual passions is too many, out of the church or in the church!

HOW VOCAL IS THE CHURCH AGAINST SOCIABLY ACCEPTABLE SELF DESTRUCTION?

A young man, addicted to narcotics once said to me, "I don't have the guts to pick up a gun and blow my *#@&^** brains out, so I'm getting the same results with drugs. They just aren't as obvious, or as fast as a gun in my mouth. Everybody I know who is abusing drugs is doing the same thing. We're all just choosing the slow way of killing ourselves." Just as "the wages of sin is death," conversely, that which works to bring death to any human being is "sin."

Fifty percent of Americans are overweight and eating themselves into an early grave. Behavior that harms persons is sin. Gluttony has been recognized as a "deadly sin" for centuries. But the modern church remains so silent that its members do not even know of their sin. Standing before fat congregations, what preacher has the courage to speak out against the lack of self-control expressed by gluttony?

Can any person have lived within the boundaries of the United States for the last couple of decades without having heard time and again that physical inactivity tends to lead to bad health and ultimately toward death? But who dares to call it sin?

When thousands of coal miners were dying of "black lung disease" a few voices appropriately rose from the church in protest against inadequate precautions by mine owners. At the same time, millions were (and still are) dying at the rate of *440,000 per year* from diseases created by the smoking cigarette. The Surgeon General speaks louder than the church against smoking, but the church does not even support him. Has anyone heard even a whisper of protest from the church against cigarette smoking? It is sociably acceptable and common in the church. Who dares to call it sin? The pastor has a family to feed and clothe. He or she knows the church would not tolerate speaking out against its sin.

When the voice of the church fails to confront sin, many churches even fail to evangelize. If a church does not recognize sin with its destructive results in both time and eternity, why would it be expected to evangelize? Why work to lead men, women, boys, girls into a saving faith relationship with God through Jesus Christ? Has a major segment of the modern church concluded with the rest of the world that trusting Christ is not really going to make any difference in people's lives? Have both the clergy and congregants lost confidence in the power of God to save? Or has the church become so self absorbed in itself that it has lost its awareness of the world's need to be saved from self-destruction?

If the thousands of sermons and sermon outlines that are available in religious book stores and on the internet are even close to representing the message of the modern church, we must conclude that the church is either blind, soundly sleeping, too frightened, or worse—it does not care. Whichever it is unbelievers of the land are being negatively impressed by much of what they see in too many of their local churches.

We who make up the church would like to believe that Christians would be viewed as the ideal example of ethical/moral lifestyle. Early in this twenty-first century, the Berna Research Group conducted a nation-wide survey of the public's attitudes toward eleven groups. They included prostitutes, lawyers, lesbians, and movie and TV performers. Non-Christians across the country rated Evangelicals tenth of the eleven, beating out only prostitutes.

I keep hearing echoes of my friend's charge, "Your Christianity isn't working."

Have we of the church not heard the charge of "irrelevance" made against us many times? Is this one of the reasons that it has been said that we have become so "heavenly minded" that we are good for nothing here on earth?

Perhaps we have become so concerned with fears of being considered legalists that we have gone to the opposite extreme—nothing seems to be worthy of being called "sin." When human beings are harmed, sin is in force. When sin in its many forms has not been confronted in societies, throughout history, great has been the fall of those societies! What voices are arising within the church to demand repentance? Some few remain. We should thank God for that portion of the church—those churches that have the courage to call sin by its real name, and raises its voice crying, "I do! I am accepting the audacious responsibility for demanding in God's behalf as did the prophet of old, 'Repent, and turn yourselves from all your transgressions, so iniquity shall not be your ruin'" (Ezekiel 18:30). Join with Jesus. Declare and continue to declare, "Repent: for the kingdom of heaven is at hand" (Mt 4:17).

Although the Christian message must confront sin, it also must proclaim grace. Good news! God still forgives!

SIN 4
FAILURE TO REPENT

I tell you…unless you repent
you will all…perish. (Lk. 13:5)

The preceding chapter closed with a lamentation for sin in the unrepentant church. However, why should we expect people to repent when sin is not condemned? Thoughtful parishioners might respond, "Repent? Repent of what?" Or they might even respond, "Repent? What do you mean?" Since the meaning of "repent" is frequently misunderstood, let's look toward a definition of repentance.

First, let's examine what repentance is *not*. Despite popular opinion, repentance is *not* simply the feeling of regret for one's sin. Although regret is a *part* of repentance, regret is not repentance. If we absolutely must use a theological word for regret, we must use the word "contrition." The Psalmist declared that "The Lord is nigh unto them that are of a broken heart; and saveth such as be of a contrite spirit" (Psalm 34:18). And again he said, "The sacrifices of God are a broken spirit: a broken and contrite heart. . ."(Ps. 51:17). One may feel contrite, (regretful) but may not follow up on the regret with a turn from sin toward God. The regret may exist as a sense of guiltiness, but millions live daily with guilt without repenting, never turning to God as the source of forgiveness and as the transformer of life. Regret may be viewed as one part of the preparation one needs to carry through with repentance.

What, then, is repentance? The transliterated Greek word for repentance is *metanoia*. Literally translated, it means "afterthought" or "change of mind." But when it is used in the New Testament it always speaks of a change of purpose that turns from sin to God. In military marching terms it may be described as an "about face" of the volition, or even more accurately, a "to the rear, March!" In highway parlance it could be described as a "U" turn away from Satan toward God—away from unrighteousness to righteousness. It is a

"U" turn of the will with the decision to obey God's law of love. It involves a turn of direction for the mind, heart, spirit, will, and attitude. When Martin Luther nailed his 95 Theses to the door of the church at Wittenburg, the first thesis read, "When our Lord and Master Jesus Christ said, 'Repent' (Matthew 4:17) he willed the entire life of believers to be one of repentance."

Changed behavior, in and of itself is not repentance. Change of behavior is the fruit of repentance. John the Baptist used precisely that language, "Bring forth fruit that is consistent with repentance (let your lives prove your change of heart)" (Matthew 3:8 AB). One of Jesus' disciples, also named John, wrote after Jesus' ascension, that lives should be so changed that they would model the life of Jesus! "Whoever says he abides in Him (Jesus) ought (as a personal debt) to walk and conduct himself in the same way in which He (Jesus) walked and conducted Himself" (1 John 2:6 AB). Jesus repeatedly invited, "Come, follow me." He was inviting His hearers to turn from the previous patterns of behavior to His. Many did. We have the names of only a few.

Repentance, as Jesus used the word, involves the recognition of one's sinfulness, and prepares the way for a turn from sin to God for salvation. However, that recognition may last only for a fleeting moment. We are so geared psychologically that we can see a truth but if that truth is painful, we can quickly hide it again from ourselves somewhere deep within the psyche. But, as carbon dioxide creates pressure within a bottle of wine, buried truth creates emotional pressure within the mind and body. These pressures (stresses), continuing over a period of time can work to create both mental illness and physical illness. The more unsavory the truth, the more it wants out. Furthermore, the more it wants out, the more energy it requires to keep it submerged.

I have envisioned a man in a swimming pool with a bunch of tennis balls. Keeping one under water is no problem. Even two or three are not difficult. But the more tennis balls he tries to keep submerged, the harder he has to work to keep them under. Over a period of time that work drains him emotionally and physically. Every "talk-therapist," whether serving under the title of Psychiatrist, Counselor, Psychologist, or Psychiatric Social Worker maintains his or her livelihood at the expense of those who have been trying to bury some unsavory truth.

During the late 1950s, when I worked out my Internship and Residency as a hospital chaplain, this inter-connection of mind, body, and spirit was a major part of our studies. During those days, our teachers had to speak of this as theory. During that period, we spoke of spiritually-emotionally generated illnesses as "psychosomatic illnesses." By the 1970s, Dr. Hans Selye was conducting research in stress laboratories in Canada with the intent of proving or disproving the theory. His monumental work has been picked up and conducted also in the United States and elsewhere.

That which we taught in former decades, we now can teach as clinically established fact. Now, no one knowledgeable in the field denies that more than one hundred different forms of physical illness can develop out of emotional stress (pressure). In recent decades, these illnesses have been called "psychogenic illnesses."

During my thirty-one years of ministry as a hospital chaplain, I conducted approximately 300,000 personal conversations among the hospital employees, my patients, and their families. I wore no clerical collar, but thousands of those with whom I conversed turned the setting into a confessional. When a bottle of wine is opened, the carbon dioxide in the wine forms tiny bubbles and immediately begins to make their way to the surface in an effort to escape. Truth also wants out! The more negative the truth, the more it wants out. When negative truth is acknowledged, emotional, physical, and spiritual healing can begin.

The elimination of confession was one of the greatest tragedies of the Protestant Reformation. Surely, no one familiar with the history of the church of the period would deny that the practice of confession was severely abused. However, large segments of the universal church went from one unhealthy extreme to another. I am reminded, in passing, that some of the gravest of evils are simply the abuse of something good.

Moses, speaking for God, instructed his people to confess their sins in preparation for offering an atoning sacrifice (cf. Leviticus 5:5). Even those immersed by John the Baptist were confessing their sins.

But "confession is for the ears of God," is the common Protestant attitude. Indeed, it is. But when a human being hears confession, God is present to hear the confession also! For those who can admit their sin to God without the presence of another human being, we can rejoice. However, most people need to confess in the presence of a human in whom God dwells. Why else would the Scripture clearly instruct, "Confess your faults one to another, and pray for one another, that you may be healed" (James 5:16). (How many Protestants can remember hearing a sermon drawn from that verse of the Bible?)

Decades ago, I sat listening to the confession of a young woman who had violated virtually every moral and ethical principle she had ever read in the Bible, heard at church, or at home. She talked a while and cried a while. Then she continued talking and stopped to continue weeping. After nearly an hour of intermittent confession and sobs, she wiped her eyes and stared strangely at me. I will never forget her words. "Chaplain Justice, this has been the strangest experience of my life. It has seemed as if you were pushed back and Jesus has been standing here between us, and I have been talking to Him." Chills traced up my spine as I realized that the two of us sat in the presence of a Third.

I asked if He had said anything to her. "Yes sir. He told me the same thing He once spoke to a woman in the Bible. He told me that He forgives me, and that I should not go back to my way of life and that I should go on my way and enjoy the life He has given me." She assured me that she had seen no vision, nor had the voice made a sound. All had been seen and heard in her mind. She was confessing to the ears of our Lord, and I was blessed by the privilege of having been present. (Since we served in the same institution, I saw her frequently in her day-to-day life over the next several years. She was enjoying a transformed life with Jesus as Her Lord. She later joined the Peace Corps and the last time I heard of her, she was serving as a missionary in Africa.)

Only when sin is confessed, is repentance possible. No one changes the course of his life until he admits that he is going in the wrong direction. Repentance turns from a disobedient style of behavior and commits to a style of behavior that is consistent with God's law. (cf. 1 Thess. 1:9).

On another occasion, a person had been deeply involved with painful confession when he paused and said, "Chaplain, I've been reading your response to what I've been telling you. If I had received the impression that you were condemning me, I would have stopped immediately. Since God is much greater than you, I've decided that if you can still accept me with all my failures, surely God can accept me." God has always accepted the repentant. Can we?

Neither John the Baptist nor Jesus held a monopoly on the call to repentance, nor was Jesus the first to introduce the concept of God's grace. Every Old Testament prophet called his people to repent—to turn from sin to God for salvation. In the Old Testament and in the New, salvation was always the response of God to those who turned from their sin to Him. Isaiah said, "Let the wicked forsake his way, and the unrighteous man his thoughts: and let him return to the Lord (*repent*), and he will have mercy upon him, . . . for he will abundantly pardon" (Isaiah 55:7). (*That's grace in the heart of the Old Testament!*)

Hear the report of God's voice to Solomon as recorded in Second Chronicles 7:14. "If my people who are called by my name humble themselves and pray, and seek my face and turn from their wicked ways, then I will hear from heaven, will forgive their sins, and will heal their land." (Here is God's call to repentance with a promise of grace that will result in their salvation.)

Someone has said that ancient, meticulous Jews detailed nine activities (not feelings) that were associated with repentance. (1) Something or someone called attention to their sin. (2) They made a decision to admit their sin. (3) Then they confessed (admitted) their sin. (4) They made a decision to turn from (discontinue) their sin. (5) They turned away from (discontinued) their sin. (6) They made a decision to turn to God—to believe that He would forgive. They would trust him enough—have enough faith in Him to accept His judgment of right and wrong over their own. (7) Then they turned to God to receive forgiveness and direction in life. (8) They made a decision to continue following God. (9) They continued following God—part of the time. Every step was preceded by a conscious decision to act.

Those who come under the ministry of Christ's church must hear the call to repent! "But how will they hear without a preacher?" (Romans 10:14) Perhaps a repentant church must be led by repentant pastors. Perhaps many ministers must first repent for having failed to demand repentance and then call for repentance by those who make up an unrepentant segment of the modern church.

However, they who call for repentance are never popular! "How dare you face us with the truth?" They stoned the prophets of old. They beheaded John the Baptist. And they crucified Jesus! Someone has said that modern man has learned how to inflict even greater pain to its prophets by simply ignoring them.

On the banks of the Jordan River, John the Baptist was preparing the people to hear Jesus when Jesus came forth to begin His ministry. Hear John blister the skin of the guilty. "You brood of vipers, who warned you to flee from the wrath to come? Therefore bring forth fruit in keeping with repentance!"

John cried out, "Repent, for the kingdom of heaven is at hand" (Matthew 3:2).

Where did Jesus start? He started with the same message that was being heralded by his cousin, John the Baptist. Jesus soon began delivering the message of the Heavenly Father, "Repent for the kingdom of heaven is at hand" (Matthew 4:17).

Mark, too, reported Jesus' demand, "The time is fulfilled (completed), and the kingdom of God is at hand; repent (have a change of mind which issues in regret for past sins and in change of conduct for the better) and believe (trust in, rely on, and adhere to) the good news (the Gospel)" (Mark 1:15 AB). Jesus sent his disciples out across the land preaching a message of repentance (cf. Mark 6:12).

Luke also reported Jesus' plea for repentance with a warning, "Except ye repent, ye shall likewise perish, *and* be lost eternally" (Luke 13:3-5 AB).

No one wants to hear a demand for repentance. Fewer are willing to repent.

Many years ago, I recently had climbed out of the cockpit of my aircraft and resigned my commission as an Air Force Officer. I had returned to Furman University to prepare for service as a Gospel Minister. I had preached fewer than a dozen sermons when the pastor of a rather large rural church invited me to preach in his absence. I had somewhat nervously delivered the message of the morning and was standing at the door of the church, shaking hands with the departing worshipers, as I had seen experienced ministers do. I had noticed one fatherly-looking gentleman standing to the side patiently waiting for others to greet me and make their parting remarks.

When the last person had filed out, he came up to me and took hold of my coat sleeve and gently tugged as he whispered, "Come over to the corner, preacher. I gotta' say something that you gotta' hear." Out of earshot of anyone who might return, in a low voice he said, "Preacher, you are a young man. You are just getting started. You'd better listen to me." I nervously waited for him to tell me of some terrible blunder I had made while filling the pulpit of their church, and wondered if he was going to recommend to the pastor that I never be permitted to preach there again. Under his breath, he whispered, "Preacher, you are going at preaching all wrong. You're trying to get people to *repent*. You're *never* going to be a popular preacher if you keep trying to get people to repent!"

I'm not sure of how far abroad his advice was heard, but it seems to have been heeded by many ministers across America. Those few voices who are calling for repentance stand as alone and as isolated as John the Baptist ever stood. After almost half a century, I am still haunted by the echoing words that my mother spoke when I told her and Dad that I was leaving the Air Force to study to become a Gospel minister. In her first moment of surprise, with wide eyes she said, "My God son! What if you lead people in the wrong direction?" In the days that followed, I realized I would never lead people in the wrong direction as long as I remained true to the teachings of my Lord, Jesus. But her haunting voice has brought chills to my spine on numerous occasions while on the platform waiting for the time to deliver a message. Many within the church are going "the wrong way." If we do not call them to repent, we are as accountable before God as we would be if we were leading them in the wrong direction. Jesus demanded repentance!

They named the sins of their people and demanded change, lest they would suffer the consequences of their sin. They called sin, sin! They spoke out against those who lied, stole, murdered, cheated in business, destroyed their newborn, and carried on adulterous affairs. The sins against which the prophets cried 3000 years ago are being practiced among people who profess to be Christians. Where are the voices of the prophets?

The Old Testament prophet was a "forthteller." He spoke forth truth. Occasionally, he "foretold" of events to come, but in keeping with the root meaning of the word, "prophet," he was always one who spoke forth in behalf of another. He spoke for God! Those who stand in the pulpits of the land are expected—even assumed to speak forth truth of the Gospel of Jesus Christ. However, many congregations worship regularly for months without hearing a message from the words of Jesus!

What are people hearing from many pulpits of America? How many voices are speaking forth for God, demanding repentance? As we have seen in the first chapter of this book, theft, rape, murder, incest, adultery, and every conceivable crime against persons and property is being enacted by members of our Lord's church who believe that they are saved!

In the midst of such evil, what is this age hearing from the American pulpit?

A common presentation of the Gospel would have us to believe that we can simply mouth the words, "I accept Jesus," and we are "saved."

Hear the voices.

"Come to Jesus!" (Without a demand for repentance and surrender to the Lordship of King Jesus that results in habitual obedience to the teachings of Christ.)

"Accept Jesus as Savior!" (Without demand for repentance and surrender to the Lordship of the Christ which includes habitual obedience to the teachings of Jesus.)

"Ask Jesus into your heart." (Without insistence on repentance and surrender to the Lordship of the Messiah which includes habitual obedience to the teachings of Christ.)

"Make a decision for Christ." (Without an accompanying decision to repent and surrender to the Lordship of Christ which includes beginning the practice of obeying the teachings of King Jesus.)

Nothing is wrong with these calls. These and similar ones are appropriate and urgently needed when they are accompanied by the clear call to repentance and surrender to the Lordship of Jesus Christ which necessitates beginning the practice of obeying the moral-ethical teachings of God's New Testament.

Several years ago, I watched one of America's most renowned evangelists as he approached people who had come forward at the "altar call" at the close of his sermon. He walked down the line tapping the heads of those waiting further instruction. I sat stunned when he stopped at one man, ceremoniously placed both hands on a man's head and screamed, "Be saved!"

People have been led into church membership saying, "Don't I have to repent? Don't I have to begin following God's teachings? Gee, that's great! I can still do as I damn well please, and I can live a lifestyle led by Satan and still be saved."

And men and women across America have been doing as they were instructed and have believed they were saved when the evidence indicates that millions remain as "lost" as souls can be. They appear to be lost in time and lost in eternity. Their lives are shambled and they are living in a self-created hell on earth.

Someone is certain to cry out against my words in distress because I may cause somebody to "doubt their salvation." Wonderful! Those who have only spoken words that say they have "accepted Christ" but have not made some significant changes in their lives, and participated in God's re-creative work in their lives *need* to question their salvation!

Another is certain to cry out that I am endangering some Christian's feelings of spiritual security in their relationship with Christ. Wonderful! ***Any relationship that is too secure tends to be neglected!*** Every one of us needs repeatedly to examine the quality of our interpersonal relationships. That certainly includes an examination of our relationship with God.

Some of the most cantankerous, mean-spirited, downright evil people on earth boast of their marvelous, close relationship with Christ. (Few pastors will disagree with me.) Although we may be thankful that only God is our final judge, we are reminded that "ye shall know them by their fruits" (Matthew 7:16). If it walks like a devil, talks like a devil, and acts like a devil, even if it thinks it is an angel, we have a strong reason to suspect that it is a devil.

My grave concern is for those who profess to be Christian, but who one day may hear, "Why do you call Me, Lord, Lord, and do not (practice) what I tell you (Luke 6:46)?

As a Marriage and Family Therapist, I long ago recognized that husbands and wives who take their relationships for granted, becoming too sure of their marital relationship, tend to neglect behaviors that help maintain a sound relationship. Then the quality of the relationship deteriorates. At least 99.99999% of the time, husband-wife relationships are damaged by destructive behaviors. Our culture would have us to believe that after feelings change, our behavior changes. Our society would have you to believe that one day your feelings of love changed, and therefore, you have changed your way of treating your spouse. WRONG! After loving behavior degenerates, the feelings degenerate! Only agapé centered love keeps a couple enjoying life together for a lifetime. And only agapé centered love keeps a person enjoying life with God for a lifetime and into eternity.

I have watched hundreds of couples rebuild their relationship with one another only by beginning habitually to work each in the other's best interests. They reestablish their relationship when they have repented (turned their behavior from negative to positive).

I know that we may not create a 100% parallel between husband-wife relationships and our relationship with God, but it is enough of a parallel to make the point. *We each must repeatedly examine the quality of our relationship with Jesus Christ. When we fail to do so, we tend to behave in ways that cause the relationship to deteriorate.*

All of us would serve ourselves well by repeatedly examining our relationship with God. However, the modern church that appears packed with an unregenerate membership dares not speak a word that would cause anyone to question his or her salvation. John MacArthur has boldly stated,

> Even the most conservative churches are teeming with people who, claiming to be born again, live like pagans. Contemporary Christians have been conditioned never to question anyone's salvation. If a person declares he has trusted Christ as Savior, no one challenges his testimony, regardless of how inconsistent his life-style may be with God's Word."[22]

Jesus never hesitated to say words that caused His hearers to question their spiritual security. He deliberately tried to destroy the expectations of life eternal held by those who were unregenerate (cf. Matt. 7:21-23). To those who assumed themselves most secure in their relationship with God, He demanded repentance!

Some questions have eternal implications. Have I repented? Have I participated with the Holy Spirit in transforming my life? (I've never seen a person recreated by God when the person was working counter to that recreation. I've never seen evidence that suggests that God ever forces *anyone* to do anything against his or her will.)

Am I accepting Christ as the Lord (the Leader, the Ruler, the King) of my life, after whom I am following daily?

If the unrepentant are saved, *from* what have they been saved, and *to* what have they been saved? We often refer to those who have been saved as having been "converted." *From* what have they been converted and *to* what have they been converted?"

Jesus insisted on a "new birth" or a "birth from above." (Jn.3:5-7). The Apostle Paul believed Jesus and also declared that the Christian is a "new creation." "Whoever is a believer in Christ is a new creation. The old way of living has disappeared. A new way of living has come into existence"(2 Cor. 5:17 GWT). The world is looking at the church and asking, "Where are all of those newly birthed, recreated people?" Non-Christians are looking for the evidence that Christ makes a difference in the Christian's life. They are looking for people whose lifestyle shows obedience to Jesus. The penman of Hebrews wrote, "And being made perfect, He (Jesus) became the author of eternal salvation *unto all them that obey him*" (Heb. 5:9)(Italics added). Hear Paul's words to Titus about his concern for "those who are defiled and unbelieving. . . . They profess that they know God but by their deeds they deny Him" (Titus 1: 15-16 NASB). When non-Christians fail to see a body of people who are obeying Jesus, they conclude that Christianity is a meaningless (non-working) religion that is little more than a body of self-righteous hypocrites. They come to our churches expecting to see the "body of Christ." They leave convinced that they have seen the "body of hypocrisy." They turn away is disgust. This is one major reason the youth of the land are jamming the church doors—to get out.

Those who profess Christianity but refuse to obey Christ contribute to the damnation of others. We of the Church insist that one who is "saved" has been "redeemed." The world is asking, "If Christians have been redeemed (set free) from what and to what have they been set free? The world is asking, "If the people of the church have been redeemed, from what were they set free? They seem as bound by the habit of gossip, deceit, spiteful actions, unethical business practices and self degrading behaviors as the rest of the world!"

J. Gerald Harris, Editor of the "Christian Index," a newspaper published primarily for Southern Baptists of the state of Georgia has written,

> A totally redeemed church could dramatically and dynamically impact our society, but how many churches are thoroughly Christian? What is a Christian? Is a Christian merely someone who believes the tenets of our faith? Is a Christian someone who willingly confesses that he or she is a believer? Is a Christian someone who has identified with a local church? The Word of God indicates that a genuine Christian is one who has been redeemed by the blood of the Lamb of God, born again, changed by the power of the cross and known by his/her fruits" (Matt 7:20).[23]

Or has "becoming a Christian" and "church membership" been lowered to nothing more than the norm for a cultured society? I once sat with an apparently refined and affluent woman whose husband laid dying in a nearby hospital room. When I asked if she had a pastor whom she might wish for me to call, she indignantly responded, "Of course, I have a pastor! Being a Christian is the only sociably acceptable thing to do!" She was not interested in seeing her pastor.

Are we really saved to a life of eternal bliss in a place called Heaven because we have filled out a card, taken the pastor's hand, possibly attended a few hours of instruction, and heard a welcoming vote by a congregation? Are we really saved to a life of eternal bliss in a place called Heaven while living on earth in a corner of hell with lust and anger that too often results in rape, sexual abuse, and murder? Are we really saved to a life of eternal bliss while living in so much greed that we inject chicken breasts, hams and other foods with water so that they will weigh more in the market? Are we truly Christian if we rob hard-working employees of their pension funds in the name of profits and good business management? Are we really saved for eternal bliss if we batter our spouses on Saturday night and sing "Oh, how I love Jesus" on Sunday?

Those who believe they are, may chill and tremble upon hearing Jesus when He said that those who enter the Kingdom of Heaven are those who do the will of the Heavenly Father (cf. Matt. 7:21). Did not Jesus go on to say that in a day of judgment He would declare, "depart from me, ye that work iniquity" (Matt. 7:23)?

Among other things, I am dually licensed by my state, both as a Professional Counselor, and as a Marriage and Family Therapist. (Since I had already earned my credentials, I went into private practice after I retired from ministry as a hospital chaplain.) At the end of the day, my wife often has asked me how the day has gone. Without giving details, on several occasions, I have heard myself reply, "Honey, I've spent the day with people who already are living in the outskirts of Hell." Their selfishness, their fussing, and bickering and outright violence have turned some homes into a corner of Hell on earth. I do not exaggerate when I say that I have sometimes wondered if I imagined it or if I could truly feel the heat of Hell and smell traces of burning sulfur in my office.

Although my understanding of a place called Hell that is beyond this mortal realm is terribly limited, experience has made it easier to believe in a literal Hell as a place of misery. I have listened too long at the bedside of my patients and to those who have turned to me for formal counseling behind closed doors to believe otherwise. During the thirty-one years I spent as a bedside hospital chaplain, some of my patients chose to talk about their physical illnesses. However, most of those with whom I conversed in that ministry took me into the "living room" of their hearts where they shared their conflicts, their hopes, their guilts, their sorrows, their successes, and their failures. I have listened to some of the most heartbreaking stories of evil that any man could hear. Surely, few men have carried more secrets than I. (I have forgotten most, and the remainder will go to the grave with me.) Much of the evil with which I have been made privy has been perpetrated by people who profess Christ as Savior.

Something's wrong! Something's wrong with a form of Christianity that makes no moral/ethical demand on the lives of its participants. It is not the message that was preached by Jesus of Nazareth. Something's wrong with a system of beliefs that promises a life of eternal bliss without surrender to the divine authority of the Christ. It is not the message preached by Jesus, the Christ. Something's wrong with a form of Christianity whose members can live in total depravity while professing to have been "born again." It is certainly not the message Jesus preached as he trod the trails and highways of Palestine. Indeed, many individuals who claim to be children of Christ, of the "household of faith" (Gal. 6:10) show evidence of belonging to the family of the devil (cf. Jn. 8:44). And by offering a cheap grace without life-changing repentance or without submission to Christ as the Lord of their lives, much of the modern church contributes to their damnation!

And Satan and his forces keep on laughing.

SIN 5
FAILURE TO SPEAK
IN A KNOWN TONGUE

Yet in the church I had rather speak
five words with my understanding that
by my voice I might teach others also than
ten thousand words in an unknown tongue. (I Cor. 14:19)

Having read the foregoing chapters you may be inclined to agree that something is terribly wrong in many North American churches. Since I spent more than forty-five years of my life in health-related ministries, I suppose it is natural for me to think in terms set by the medical model. When physicians have diagnosed an illness, they want to treat the cause—not to treat only the symptoms.

The "cause" of the sickness in dying churches is nothing less than sins of both, omission and commission, practiced by both, the members and the clergy (of which I am one). Some who read these pages are old enough to remember Pogo, a comic strip 'possum from the Louisiana swamps. I remember the time Pogo found reason to peek around a cypress tree and exclaim, "We has found the enemy! They is us!" We, who want most to promote the Kingdom of God, also may be among those most responsible for holding back the advance of the Kingdom of God.

Several years ago, I was talking with a warm acquaintance after he had attended public worship for only the third or fourth time in his life. Sounding frustrated, he said, "Bill, most of the time, I didn't know what the preacher was talking about. He seemed to be talking in a language I didn't understand. I've got a college degree, but he used a lot of words I've never heard before in all my life. Many of the words I thought I understood seemed to have a different meaning to him than they had for me. I came away wondering what he had said."

A professor of my seminary years occasionally referred to the "stained glass language of Zion" that we preachers tend to use in the pulpit. In the classroom, we smiled with understanding. I'm not smiling as I think of my own abuse of the "stained glass language of Zion." It was during those seminary years that I drove past a church and read a large sign in its yard: "Consecration Sunday!" I felt vaguely guilty when I read that sign. What did that word "consecration" mean? I had a better formal education than most people. I had been in Sunday School and worshiped in my church regularly since I was age three. I had read the Bible from cover to cover. I had majored in religion while earning a Bachelor's Degree from a highly reputable university. The Air Force had provided me with more than a year of classroom instruction while preparing me to pilot heavy bombers. I was in my second year of a three-year seminary Master's Degree program. However, I was not certain that I knew the meaning of the word "consecration" on that sign.

I had heard it occasionally all my life. My Sunday School teachers had used it. My pastors had used it. I had read it in the Bible, but I had always depended on the context in which it was used to conclude its probable meaning. No one had ever defined it to me, and I had never taken the trouble to look it up in a dictionary. This time, I was to find no peace until I had turned to a dictionary of theological terms. When I discovered that the word "consecration" was nothing more than a fifty-cent word for "dedication," I smiled smugly while thinking, "I was correct in my earlier conclusions, but now I know for certain what it means. Now, I, too, can confidently use the word."

Then I thought, "But Bill, you are blessed with the privilege of having earned a far better formal education than most people, and you had to look it up in a theological dictionary to know its meaning for certain. You are about to perpetuate an unknown language. People won't understand you!"

Years passed. I graduated from seminary, completed three and one half years of internship and residency in training to serve as a hospital chaplain, and was teaching a course in "Religion and Nursing" in our hospital's accredited school of nursing. During a lecture, one day, I used the word "grace." On a whim, I asked everyone to tear off half a sheet of paper and write a definition of the word I had just used—"grace."

Back in my office, I sat dismayed to find that not one answer was complete enough to be considered correct. When I had used a word commonly used in pulpits across the country and in Sunday School classrooms of virtually every church, my students had not understood me when I had used the word "grace" in my lecture to them. I wondered, "What other words are in my 'preacher's vocabulary' that are not understood when I use them in the classroom and in the pulpit?"

Over the next several days, I put together a list of theological words commonly spoken in Christian pulpits. The collection included the words "grace," "repent," "bless," "redeem," "incarnation," and "consecrate." I did not have the courage ask them to define the words, "expiation," "propitiation," "sanctification," "atonement," "Christ," or "vicarious." Back in the classroom, I asked them to write the following statement, "I have been under what I consider to be the strong influence of organized Christianity for _____ years (fill in the blank.)" I explained that I was not talking about the day-to-day cultural influence, but was talking about their attendance in Sunday School, in regular public worship, and other direct influences on their understanding of Christianity. Then I asked them to define the words I had selected. The definitions were alarmingly inadequate!

Over the next ten years, I conducted the same survey among all incoming students into our program for Nurse Training. I promised to cut off the names from their papers after I knew that everyone had submitted their answers. Before I tell you the results, let me tell you more about those who participated in the survey.

As students in an accredited school of nursing, they all were high-school graduates and well above the average intelligence level. All were Protestant, mostly Southern Baptists, and with few exceptions, they had been under the strong educational influence of organized Christianity for fifteen to twenty years. They represented churches both large and small. In brief, they represented Protestant Christianity in the heart of the Bible Belt of the United States. Although the survey could not be called a scientific statistical study, it revealed enough to point out a major factor contributing to the sickness of the modern church.

Let's take a brief overview of the results.

- What were the typical definitions for the word, "grace"—a word liberally sprinkled throughout a large percent of our sermons and religious discussion? The following are representative samples of the answers.
  "Grace is mercy."
  "Grace is trust."
  A blessing neither given nor received"
  "The blessing one gets"
  "Above human powers in spirituality"
  "Divine presence"
  "Something that God has"

Are these answers totally wrong? No, but what knowledgeable person would call them correct? Fewer than one in ten gave an answer comparable to "unmerited or undeserved favor."

- How did they define the word, "repent?"
  "Confess your sins and be truly sorry"
  "To be forgiven"
  The most typical type of answer read, "To be truly sorry for one's sins and seek forgiveness from God."

Again, the answers lack the most vital element required to accurately define "repentance." Only about five percent made reference to the vital ingredient in repentance given by the first student to take the survey: "To change from a previous trend of life to a better trend." Even fewer made reference to the change of mind, and will.

- How did they respond to the word "bless)—perhaps the most overused and least understood word in Christian jargon?
  "To show mercy"
  "To keep in God's realm of being"
  "Take care of—protect"
  "To give a reward to someone"
  "Make good come out of something"
  "Bestow feeling"

The essential elements of "approval" or "happiness" were rare among the responses.

- The word "redeem" is frequently used by evangelical Christians. How did my students define it?
  "To make a person acceptable to God"
  "Saved or given watch or concern over"
  "Cleanse again"
  "To start a new life by giving meaning to the old one"
  "To make good, or to get the worth of something"

Although the word "forgive" was occasionally used, only once did I ever see the essential words "set free" among the responses.

- Although several students left the space blank after the word "consecration" not many had any real trouble with it. Some responded with statements similar to, "Brought to God" and "Repent of sin," but about ninety percent used the word, "devoted" or "dedicated" in their answers.

- My student's response to one word on my list gave me the biggest surprise of all. "Define the word, 'Incarnation' as it is commonly used among Christians." Five years passed before I received the first correct definition! Five years passed before the first student said that the Incarnation refers to the presence of God on earth in human flesh. There were no typical responses. Here are a few random samples.
  "Change from an old nature to a new nature"
  "To be born again"
  "Death outside of Christ"
  "To live in Christ"
  "New life"
  "Change in body"

The meaningless list could go on and on. Many students were so lost for an answer that they left the space blank.

When I have asked my students why they were so lacking in understanding the words they have heard used in church all their lives, repeatedly, I received the same answers: "We've heard them many times, but nobody has ever defined them for us." "We have concluded their meanings based on how they were used within the context of what was being said." "They were words we heard only at church. We didn't need them at any other time, so we never took the trouble to look them up in a dictionary at home." Those few who had tried to find some of the words in a dictionary complained that they seemed to have a different meaning at church than when used elsewhere.

Ministers and church educators who have been courageous enough to conduct a similar survey in their own churches have been startled by the degree of ignorance among even those who have been members of the church for many years.

However relevant, vital, and meaningful our words may be, if they are not understood, they are of no value to anyone! The church is sinning according to one of the most foundational meanings of the word, "sin." When we go back to the words the New Testament used for "sin," we find a word borrowed from the field of battle. When a soldier shot at a target and the arrow *fell short of the mark* or *missed the mark* (the "bulls eye"), he had "sinned."

We of the church may be aiming generally in the right direction, but when we are using a language that few understand, we are *missing the mark* and millions are being misled by what they *think* they are hearing. Even more continue walking in paths of unrighteousness because of what they are *not* hearing. They may not have "ears to hear."

You may protest, "But they are good words. They are *Biblical* words."

65

Yes, they are. But no matter how Biblical they are, they are not being understood! Even if God were to write them in the sky, if they were not understood, they would be meaningless without an interpreter! When a message was written on the wall of King Balshazzar's castle, they meant nothing to the king until Daniel interpreted them for him in a language that the king understood (Dan. 5:5-28).

Theological jargon has its use, among those who understand it. Every profession has a professional jargon. The "stained glass language of Zion" is the professional language of the Gospel Minister. However, professional jargon is to be used only among those who clearly understand it.

Physicians are sometimes criticized for using long, strange-sounding words and phrases that their patients do not understand. On numerous occasions, when I have listened to a physician use language that brought quizzical expressions to the face of patient or family, I have suggested to the physician that he or she define the illness or treatment in simple language.

When I was a young man, working with a construction gang, we "hammered cat-heads," reinforced the underside of concrete forms with "stiff-knees" and we "tied re-bar" to "highchairs." The first time I told my girlfriend I had been hammering cat-heads most of the day, she looked at me as if to ask, "What on earth are you talking about?"

A few years later while I was serving as an Air Force Pilot flying four-engine bombers (B-29 Superfortresses) I often "trimmed tabs," "dropped flaps," "chopped throttles," and "feathered props." On one occasion, when I came home from a flight and found visitors, I explained that I was late because we had "lost an engine" between Iwo Jima and Okinawa. A visitor looked horrified. She had envisioned an engine breaking loose from the aircraft and plummeting into the Pacific Ocean. I tried to correct her misunderstanding, but I further confused her when I explained that "a jug had overheated" and we had been forced to "chop the throttle" and "feather the prop" to keep the engine from "wind-milling." She did not look satisfied. I was speaking a language that was perfectly clear in my mind and would have been clear to the mind of any flyer who was familiar with multi-engine propeller-driven aircraft. I was using the "in" language—the jargon of flyers of that period. To her ears, I was speaking in an unknown tongue. She was no flyer and needed me to interpret. For her to understand, I needed to describe what had happened in plain, everyday language.

The "stained glass language of Zion," the "preacher's jargon" has its place among the "professional clergy" and others who clearly understand it, but to the typical man and woman in the pew or church classroom, it is an unknown tongue. To them, we must use plain, simple, everyday English, or they will go away shaking their heads and wondering, "What on earth was the minister saying?"

The Apostle Paul spoke clearly to this issue. He was not talking only about glossolalia when he said that he would rather speak five words that were understood than ten thousand words that were not (1 Cor. 14:19). Paul saw the presentation of the Gospel as too important to be spoken in a language his hearers did not understand.

Someone has suggested that we need to teach our "stained glass language" to the people in the pew, or perhaps we need to establish a new catechism. If we do that, the church still will be talking to itself. "Outsiders" will remain outsiders. The occasional worshiper will come and go and will have heard little we have said. The burden is on those of us who proclaim the Gospel to speak in the plain language of the people.

Or am I lifting the corner of the cover to an issue that smells even worse than the one already under discussion. Do *we* know what we are talking about? Might we be using the high-sounding theological jargon as a cover for our own ignorance? Do we, the speakers, know the meaning of the words we are using? If we *can't* use plain language to say what we mean, that tells us that we have some hard study ahead. We may be among the blind who are leading the blind. Many may need to make a list of their theological vocabulary and then study the words until they can speak the profound truths of the Gospel in language people understand.

The pulpit and the church classroom are the only sources of Biblical truth for most Americans. This, which is often called a "Christian Nation," is profoundly ignorant of Biblical truth. George Gallup has been conducting surveys across America for many years. He has concluded that one half of all Americans do not know that Geneses is the first book of the Bible. One third do not know who delivered the "Sermon on the Mount." (Many believe it was delivered by Billy Graham.) A full 25% do not know what is celebrated at Easter. Six of ten cannot name five of the Ten Commandments. A few weeks ago, I was talking with a man in his sixties who spent many years in the church before turning away. He was surprised to learn that the word "gospel" means "good news."

Is there no sin in such ignorance?

For the sake of the world around us, the church must repent by turning from its use of a language that people do not understand and by turning to the habitual use of the language of the home and the workplace. For the sake of the world around us, the church must work to improve the teaching-learning process of those who come under our ministry. The teacher has not taught if the learner has not learned.

Across America, secular educators are working feverishly to upgrade the teaching-learning process in our public and private schools by use of digital technology that includes interactive studies at computer terminals. Industry is using presentation software to educate employees at all levels.

This week, hundreds of thousands of Sunday School teachers will walk into their classrooms to teach both children and adults with the same teaching methods that their ancestors were using to teach hundreds of years ago. Can the church afford to remain in the seventeenth century with its teaching methods when so many of those who attend do not understand what they are hearing?

SIN 6
FAILURE TO LIVE PEACEABLY
UNDER THE PRINCE OF PEACE

If it is possible, *so far as
it depends on you,* live
peaceably with all. (Rom. 12:18)

Late in 1953, the Korean War had ended and military men and women in the Far Eastern Theater of Military Operations were beginning to enjoy the terms of an uneasy "peace" (merely a period without fighting). The armistice had been signed at Panmunjeom on July 27, 1953, but a problem related to the release of prisoners of war threatened the renewal of hostilities. Those of us who were aware, gazed into the abyss of an all out nuclear war.

We who flew combat aircraft learned that war could again erupt any moment and that if it did, we were going to strike an earth-shaking blow at the heart of "Red China." We knew that we would be initiating the third world war. Every aircraft in the Strategic Air Command was readied to strike. My own B-29 Superfortress bomber was loaded to the maximum with ammunition for all twelve fifty caliber machine guns, and in our bomb-bays hung twenty thousand pounds of bombs. With assigned targets inside the Chinese mainland, and nuclear weapons in the bomb bays of some of our aircraft, we knew that if fighting erupted, we would be the first to die in combat while initiating World War III. We reminded ourselves that we were simply coping with the same sort of feelings experienced by every man or woman who has ever waited in the final minutes before going into battle. For more than a week, we waited. We all wished we could feel safe again in the arms of our families back home.

During those troubled times, some of us found solace in public worship off the military post in an Okinawan village. Worship was led by a missionary who had returned to Okinawa after having recovered from wounds received there during that island's invasion near the end of WWII. He had caught a piece of shrapnel in his throat, which left him with a terrible speech impediment. During his recovery, he felt that our Lord was calling him back to Okinawa to preach the Gospel among the native Okinawans and the military personnel stationed there. Because of his speech deficiency, his denomination rejected him for foreign mission work. As he expressed it, "My denomination said 'No,' but my Lord still said, 'Go,' so I came with an independent missionary group." He had joined the Navigators.

We called our Saturday evening worship period, "the GI Gospel Hour." Through my missionary friend, I became acquainted with missionary families of several Protestant denominations. When the peace became more secure, we disarmed our aircraft of bombs and ammunition.

After a while, several of us began working to create an Okinawan Christian Association. No group could have been more mixed. Airmen, soldiers, sailors, officers and enlisted men, male and female, black, white and native Americans, Japanese, Okinawans, a Hispanic, Baptists, Methodists, Presbyterians, Church of God, Full Gospel, Four Square Gospel, Nazarene, non-denominational Christians, and members of denominations of which I had never heard, all joined efforts. The goal was simple: to promote the Kingdom of God on Okinawa. We were interested in working cooperatively for anything that would promote the cause of Christ on Okinawa and the outlying islands.

When one small mission began plans to promote an effort, a nearby missionary or local church leader immediately asked, "How can I help?" Everyone worked as a unified body in efforts to expand and nurture the family of God. No one ever seemed to think in terms of denominational differences. We were simply Christians.

When a Southern Baptist missionary arrived on the island, he began to set up a tent in a village. "No. No," said a missionary from another denomination and local church leaders. "You are welcome to use our mission. How else can we help?" A year later, he had never unpacked his tent, having been welcomed by local church leaders to use their facilities for all of his missionary efforts.

It was in this atmosphere that I began to sense God's claim on my life to serve in some form of a full-time Christian ministry. My plans to return to civilian life and become a commercial air line pilot, or to complete my studies in Construction Engineering were set aside as I realized that if I were to live at peace with my Lord and myself, I had to become a Gospel Minister.

Back in the States, I resigned my commission as an Air Force officer and began studying for ministry. Having lived in the Orient for two years, my "culture shock" upon returning to the U.S. was not really cultural. It was spiritual. I'm not certain that I have recovered after more than fifty years.

Where was the bond of unity among Christian brothers and sisters? Denominational lines were drawn, sometimes as if they were battle lines. When I visited to worship in a church of a denomination different from my own, I was startled when the pastor "suggested" that since I was of a different denomination, I should leave before they served communion. (I had never even heard of "closed communion.")

By this time, I had become aware of hostility of many Christians against non-Christians. When the Christian learned that the non-Christian disbelieved the divinity of Jesus Christ or that the non-Christian disbelieved in the existence of God, the person found himself or herself under verbal assault. I've never seen or even heard of anyone entering a faith relationship with Christ by fiery-eyed, angry-voiced, clinched-fisted efforts at evangelism. One young man told me recently that he has been verbally attacked so many times that he has begun to prepare to defend himself any time someone learns that he is a non-believer. This hostile attitude is more in keeping with the attitude any people have accused Moslems of holding!

Then, I was sometimes stunned when leaders of one denomination condemned other denominations. Pastors spoke with thinly veiled hostility against denominations of fellow believers. Having interacted regularly with Christians of all denominations on Okinawa, I began attending meetings of the local Interdenominational Ministerial Association. By the end of the first meeting, I felt overwhelmed by the hostile environment! Ecumenical brotherhood had been executed by stoning long ago before I arrived. I kept thinking, "Something's wrong. Where is the spirit of love and brotherhood among Christians that I had enjoyed on Okinawa?" (Few women were permitted to minister in "main-stream" denominations in those days. Men were too hostile against the thought of women in ministerial roles.) I kept asking, "Where is the love that my Lord had commanded of the citizens of the Kingdom of God." My wife called to my attention that when I came home in the evening after having attended a meeting of the Ministerial Association that I always had a headache. When I quit attending, my headaches disappeared. The environment of the Ministerial Association was making me sick! My disease had been taking the form of disease.

However, that hostility was mild when compared to the hostility directed toward ministers within their own denominations. Everyone seemed to have identified with a "theological camp." Most who were disinterested in fighting had learned that he who takes no side gets shot at from all sides. Some anticipated breakups of some of the nation's largest denominations because of "pre-millinial," "post-millinial," and "a-millinial" theological stances related to the timing of Christ's return. During that time, I became so intimately familiar with each of the theological stances that I could debate

71

in favor of any one of the three. I could then turn around and shoot holes in my own argument. Similar to the way war-arousing issues change between nations great and small, the issues of the church also change with time. Few continue for more than a decade. However, the same mean spirits live on. (Only yesterday, my pastor mentioned the newest that looms on the horizon. It, too, shall pass away.)

Some of the bloodiest wars fought in history have been civil wars. But having lived through three great wars and the ever-continuing four thousand year old conflict in the Middle East, I have seen nothing civil about any war.

In 64 B.C. Caesar Augustus became Emperor of the Roman Empire with world peace as one of his goals. He soon had a reason to feel proud of the Pax Romana: the Roman Peace. The people were so pleased with his success at maintaining peace throughout the Empire that they soon dubbed him "The Prince of Peace," and after he died, they declared him a god. We Christians can appropriately refer to our Lord Jesus Christ as the true Prince of Peace, while we, His subjects keep fighting bitter battles with one another. Too many put more energy into fighting one another than into fighting the true enemy—the forces of Satan.

When brothers fight brothers, they tend to be vicious. As a young minister, I learned that gossip among ministers was brutal. "Badmouthing" of brother ministers began to seem characteristic as I tried to adjust to my new "Christian" climate. But criticism among the ministers seemed endless. Our New Testament teaches, "Speak not evil one of another, brethren. He that speaketh evil of his brother, and judgeth his brother, speaketh evil of the Law" (James 4:11). Attempting to justify ill will, some have declared, "Anyone who believes like he does is not my brother." Someone has accurately said, "Rarely does a man do wrong without first justifying his actions to himself." Unfortunately, when a person justifies himself, he sees no need for Christ to justify him.

Then I began to see that ministers tend to be afraid of one another. They fear being wounded by their brother's criticism. Therefore, when a minister is hurting, he rarely has a confidant in ministry with whom he can safely share his pain or think through a solution to a problem. One pastor and his wife drove more than 600 miles each week to see me for marriage counseling for fear that some other minister in town would learn that they needed marriage counseling. Another pastor and his wife drove more than 500 miles twice a week while working out their marital conflicts.

When I began attending denominational conventions, I began to see and hear the kind of conflict that one might expect to encounter at any other political convention. Only the "smoke-filled rooms" for election planning were missing. (I should more accurately say that the smoke was missing from the rooms where men planned election campaigns.) Hostile exchanges on the convention floor were matched by hostile tones spewing from huddled groups in the corridors. "Is there no sin here?" I wondered, "have the words of 1 John 4:20 been forgotten? ". . . he that loveth not his brother whom he hath seen, how can he love God whom he hath not seen?" John issued more warnings, "We know that we have passed from death unto life, because we love the brethren. *He that loveth not his brother abideth in death"* (1 John 3:14). Many years before I retired, I quit attending denominational conventions. I could not tolerate the pain.

In my mind, I see an unfunny science fiction cartoon that seems burned into my memory. The first frame depicted soldiers in combat gear prepared to attack giants from outer space that were indiscriminately killing the helpless citizens of a village. The next frame showed soldiers with rifles raised to their shoulders while others pointed other deadly weapons toward the evil giants. Somewhere between this frame and the final frame, a civil war had erupted. The final frame showed the soldiers shooting one another while the citizens looked on with horror and the monsters smile while they continued to devour more screaming victims.

Across America, citizens are being devoured by monstrous hatred, poverty, lust, greed and injustice while the warriors deplete their energies by fighting one another in an unholy, uncivil war. Angry radical Moslem terrorists have crashed airplanes into tall buildings, killing innocent and helpless victims in the name of Allah. America declared a "War on Terrorism."

However, when angry Ku Klux Klan terrorists have bombed and burned churches killing innocent and helpless victims in the name of Jesus Christ, Americans declared no war on terrorism, and the church remained virtually silent. All the while, it sang, "Onward Christian Soldiers," but the "soldiers of the cross" were busy shooting one another with bitter words. Gigantic enemies continue to destroy throughout the land.

Although the numbers have dropped, each year, 25,000 Americans still die in alcohol-related traffic accidents. During the Vietnam War 58,000 Americans were killed over a ten-year period. Many of the clergy led marches in the streets to protest the killing. During the same ten-year period, 274,000 Americans were slaughtered in alcohol-related traffic accidents. No one led protest marches in the streets. At the turn of the century, alcohol-related accidents were costing $46,000,000,000 (that's forty-six *Billion* dollars) per year. And alcohol was responsible for at least 100,000 deaths per year from various other alcohol-related causes. Victim's families have shed barrels of tears. The monster destroys its victims and their families while the "soldiers" shoot hostile, damaging words at and about one another.

In 2008, a study found that the cost of treating seven common chronic illnesses resulting from Cigarette smoking: cancer, diabetes, hypertension, stroke, heart disease, pulmonary conditions and mental illness, which together affect a total of 109 million U.S. residents—is costing at least $277 *billion* per year. Medical costs alone place the ultimate financial cost of cigarettes at $7.18 per pack! The cost of lost productivity amounts to about 1.1 trillion dollars.

Several years ago, I read somewhere that half of the general hospital beds in the U.S. were filled with patients who were ill largely because of cigarette smoking. I thought that sounded unreasonably high. "Somebody's mistaken."

Since I was a hospital chaplain, I knew our patients quite well. I sat down with a pencil and pad and began a mental survey of our currently occupied beds. When I had finished my count, I was truly surprised. Almost exactly half of our patients appeared to have been admitted because of illnesses in which cigarettes were a contributing factor.

As if physical illness and economic costs were not enough, in the first decade of the twenty-first century, each year more than 440,000 persons are dieing prematurely because they smoked cigarettes. Most die in the clutches of destructive addictive chemicals more powerful than their own will. Addictive substances in cigarettes have remained legal, while we focus almost exclusively on the use of illegal drugs used by our youth.

If adults can keep attention focused on the youth, perhaps attention can remain distracted from the 14,000,000 adult users of illegal drugs. Between 1989 and 1998, American users spent $39 billion to $77 billion yearly on cocaine and $10 billion to $22 billion yearly on heroin. The "Drug Czar" John P Walters, Director of National Drug Control Policy reported in a White House Release that early in the twenty-first century cocaine, heroin, and other illegal drugs are costing the U.S. economy 160 billion dollars each year. He added that illegal drugs are "a direct threat to the economic security of the United States."

Whether the addictive substance is packaged as a cigarette, or as a plastic envelope of marijuana, cocaine, ecstasy, OxyContin (a beneficial drug taken to the street), or any of a host of other drugs used illicitly, they are destructive to human beings. And if they are destructive to human beings, their use is sinful!

All addictions are not to substances taken into the body. Studies that include Harvard University and Gamblers Anonymous result in reports that estimate that between 12,000,000 and 15,400,000 Americans are addicted to gambling. These are not affluent people. Indeed, the average compulsive gambler has debts averaging $80,000.

A New York lottery agent has stated that 70% of those who purchase his tickets are poor black, or Hispanic. Anyone who has looked at the issue knows that the poor wager a larger percentage of their income than do the more affluent. Those who can least afford to gamble any part of their income tend to be those who wager the most on the lottery, sports events, automobile and dog or horse races.

Although I have never wagered one penny on the internet, advertisements for internet casinos have appeared on the screen of my computer several times each week. In the early twenty-first century, approximately 1,400 web sites encourage gambling. Accustomed to playing computer games, children use the computer to surf into the gambling arena. Ninety-six percent of those who become addicted to gambling began before age fourteen. Those not introduced to gambling by the internet casinos are enticed by the state lotteries. Knowing that they are seven times more likely to be killed by lightening than they are of winning a million dollars in a state lottery means little to them. Of course, promoters of state lotteries have claimed great overall economic benefits. However, gambling depresses business by diverting money from the capital economy into the gambling industry, which does nothing to stimulate the economy. This money diverted from the capital economy amounts to nearly $300 billion yearly. This is over $70 billion more than is spent annually on the elementary and secondary educational system in the United States. Gambling losses further deplete the economy by increasing costs to the state from bankruptcies, to addiction treatment centers, to increased crime, and to the penal system.

The state of Connecticut has concluded that casinos appear to be magnets for crime. In 1997, the State Police Casino Operations Unit investigated over 800 casino-related crimes. In 1999 they investigated over 1,000 crimes that included rape, murder, larceny, and automobile thefts.

Although the church has often stood in opposition to the introduction of legalized gambling, its voice has remained almost silent after gambeling has been legally authorized. Therefore, many regular worshipers have not been informed that gambling is sin.

Although gambling promotes materialism and often robs families of money that should be spent on family needs, gambling has a foundational principle that violates the most basic teaching (command) of Jesus Christ. Jesus' "Law of Love" requires that his followers must work in the best interests of other persons. Gambling seeks to gain by the neighbor's loss.

During almost any discussion of gambling, someone is likely to suggest that all business is a gamble. Of course, when one enters a business enterprise, he or she runs the risk of losing the investment, while hoping to gain from their investment. One runs the risk of losing the investment. However, no one "wins" as a result of the loss. In a legitimate business enterprise, the seller of an item or service and the buyer of that item or service simply make a trade. Money exchanges for the item or service. No one looses. Both win.

However, if I bet five dollars on a lottery ticket, I am hoping that millions of other people lose their investment while I gain the money they have invested. In a true gamble, someone wins at the expense of another (or even millions of others). Therefore, gambling in any form violates Jesus command to love as He loves (John 13:34). Instead of promoting the best interests of others, gambling robs from the best interests of others, often working to destroy them. The bankruptcies, divorces, and suicides attest to its destructiveness. Even a 16 year-old boy attempted suicide after losing $6,000 on lottery tickets.

The giants continue to destroy, and "Christian soldiers" still shoot at one another and rarely speak from their pulpits against the sin of the people.

The gigantic sins called murder, forcible rape, robbery, aggravated assault, and arson all increased during the turn of the century. Only truly regenerated hearts can accomplish what our prison system has failed to accomplish. *One of every 147 Americans is now confined in prison.* Four children in ten now live in one-parent homes. Suicide is the second leading cause of teen deaths in the U.S.

In the American holocaust, approximately 1,300,000 deaths by abortion are performed each year, averaging more than 3,500 abortions on each day of the year. Statisticians cannot agree on the number of abortions performed since the Supreme Court Roe V. Wade in 1973. However, their estimates range between 40,000,000 and 45,000,00 as the number of deaths by abortion since 1973. That number of fetal executions equals approximately one third of the number of people who populated the United States in 1943. Protestant women account for 43% of those abortions and 27% identify themselves as Catholics. Gigantic evils are destroying our people! After reading these figures, and considering that "the pill" was introduced in the early 1970s, we might expect a decline in the number of births to unmarried women. Wrong! The numbers of births to unmarried women rose slowly each year from the early 1940s (less than 4% of all births in 1942) until the early 1970s. After the introduction of "the pill" and the broad legalization of abortions, the percentages of births to unmarried women began to rapidly increase each year accounting for 35.7% of all births in 2008.

Is there any servant of the Gospel of Jesus Christ who does not hurt as he or she watches human beings already sweating over the flames of Hell, with satanic forces dragging more into their torture chambers every day? Although we do not all agree in our theological persuasions, we share common concerns. Though we do not all agree on battle tactics, we have *one common foe*. Have we forgotten who he is? He is *not* a brother. The Bible's first reference to him called him a subtle serpent. You may know him as Satan. You might even insist that the enemy is really the dark side of each individual. The Bible speaks of him as a destructive personality. (Shall we stop and fight here?) Can we afford the time and energy to fight unending, un-winnable battles among ourselves?

In the year 1517, the whole church began a terrible struggle: the Protestant Reformation. God has always been able to salvage good from out of the worst of man's actions. For both Roman Catholics and Protestants, He has salvaged good.

Since the Reformation, hundreds of less dramatic, but significant divisions have been created among the world-wide body of believers. However, virtually all have grown out of hostile attitudes among brothers and sisters. Dr. David B. Barrett, et. el., in the *World Christian Encyclopedia, Second Edition,* counts 33,830 Christian denominations. Yes, the number is thirty-three thousand eight hundred thirty distinctively different denominations! The list probably will need to be updated to include a new one within the months ahead. We have more than 300 in the United States today. Who could count the thousands of "independent" churches that refuse to align with any denomination? The "Church's One Foundation" stands firm, but its "structure" is crumbling.

With few exceptions, if any, each new denomination has formed out of a hostile environment. Have we so totally closed our ears to Christ's commandment to love that the battle for a religious dogma and/or individual egotistical pride is more important than love among brothers and sisters in Christ? Many expend so much time and energy fighting one another that they have neither the time nor the energy for carrying out the Great Commission. They are too exhausted to work at making disciples of Jesus Christ wherever they are going into the world.

In the fashion of denominational splits, so also split individual churches. Although I can find no statistical data, I suspect that *at least* ninety percent of all new churches form out of a hostile division among church members. This appears to be one of our "dirty little secrets" within the church. In an effort to find reliable statistics on the subject, I searched the internet. When I found nothing, I contacted several pastors. When they could give no figures, I contacted Professors of Church Growth in two large post-graduate institutions for training ministers. They knew of no available statistics and knew no one who might know of them. What denominational headquarters wants the world to know the high percent of new churches that have formed as the results of fights among their own people? Can we blame them for burying such smelly information?

Efforts to "plant" new churches in communities that need them stand as the ideal New Testament model for establishing new churches. While some churches build reputations for splitting amid anger, some few have built reputations for joyfully and peacefully dividing so they can create new churches. During my period of study at the Southern Baptist theological seminary in New Orleans, I served as the Associate Pastor of the St. Charles Avenue Christian Church. Of course, we had our theological differences. However, we comfortably focused on our commonality: our love for our Lord Jesus.

It was a church with a reputation. They were known for their dedication to "church planting." In recent years, they had established three new churches in regions of New Orleans that needed a new church. Each time the St. Charles Avenue church grew numerically strong enough, after much planning, a group left to establish a new church while receiving the full emotional, spiritual and financial support of the St. Charles Avenue body of believers. When the new group arrived in the new community, they did not sit inside their meeting place and wait for the community to come to them. In keeping with Christ's Great Commission, they worked throughout the community to make disciples. When that church got strong enough, they were expected to divide and create another new church. The St. Charles Avenue church enjoyed being not only a "mother church" but a "grandmother church." They did not have the time, energy, or inclination to fight. They had a more important passion. They had a mission to conduct!

They did not always agree. However, they had learned to disagree agreeably. I learned that some debate had occurred about calling me, a minister of a different denomination, to serve their church. Where and when to establish a new church invited serious discussion and disagreement, but they could discuss issues in a friendly atmosphere.

We would like to believe that if churches are going to fight and divide, they would do so on major issues of the faith. Some do, but more often, they are over personal, selfish, self-centered issues among vindictive members.

In my limited personal knowledge of church fights, I know of three different churches that have divided because of *differences of opinion about the location of the musical instruments.* (If it were not evil, it would sound humorous.) In each of the three, one group wanted the organ on the right of the pulpit and the piano on the left. The other group wanted the piano on the right of the pulpit and the organ on the left. Is there no immorality in such flagrant violations of King Jesus' command to love one another? In each of the situations, non-Christians of the region snickered and wagged their heads. I suspect Satan laughed aloud.

Church fights usually accomplish at least one thing. They turn souls away from a saving faith relationship with Jesus Christ. I recall a conversation with an elderly woman who firmly rejected Christ and seriously questioned the reality of the existence of a God. In parting, I suggested that she might, at least, attend the church in her community. Her eyes widened and her brow wrinkled as she exclaimed, "Why would I want to go there? I sit at home on my little hill and live in peace with my neighbors. All they do at that church is fight! They haven't got sense enough to keep their dirty laundry out of the community. Why would I want to subject myself to that atmosphere?" I did not blame her. I don't like that kind of atmosphere, either.

Historians tell us that in an era gone by, when the world was struggling with famine, ignorance, war, and pestilence, the church was caught up in heated debate about how many angels could dance on the head of a pin.

Will historians of the future describe our era as a time when the people were being consumed by monstrous evils, and the "soldiers of the cross" were shooting and wounding one another? The on-looking world stands aghast. Atheists sneer. Satan laughs. And I suspect that Christ weeps—again.

SIN 7
FAILURE TO ABSTAIN
FROM IDOLATRY
(THE GOD IN THE MIRROR)

...thus says the Lord God, Repent
and turn yourself from your idols;
and turn away your faces from
all your abominations. (Ezek. 14:6)

From the dawn of human history, men have created gods. A worn adage reminds us that on the sixth day of creation, God created man, and from that time on man has been creating gods. The farther man has moved from creating tangible images of gods, the stronger his efforts to make God fit into his own desired image. The Persians, Babylonians, Egyptians, Assyrians, Greeks, and Romans had their gods by the hundreds with household idols in the millions. Archeologists have found so many that currently, in the early part of the twenty-first century, we can purchase those ancient relics from large archeological collectors for as little as one hundred fifty dollars each.[24]

The gods that men worship have long held my fascination. In Bangkok, I stood in awe before the magnificent carving atop a column in the Temple of the Emerald Buddha. A few blocks away I saw the hundred-foot-long Reclining Buddha, and hundreds of other marvelously fashioned statues of the god.

From a Singapore antique shop, I brought home a small 600 year old head of Buddha and an eighteen-inch tall intricately carved wooden god from Java. That idol depicts a little man sitting on the shoulders of a figure with the head, wings, tail-feathers, and feet of a bird with the hands, arms, legs and torso of a man. The right foot grasps a serpent by the throat.

I've reflected at a shrine to the "god of the sea" on a beach of the island of Okinawa.

I've gazed upon the beetle gods, the cat gods, the jackal gods, and Taweret, the goddess of fertility and childbirth of the ancient Egyptians. I've admired the beauty of the golden image of Matt, the goddess of truth, which was believed to regulate the seasons, movement of the stars and the relationships between mortal man and the gods.

Ancient idols have taken the form of virtually everything from snakes, goats, and bulls, to images of well-endowed human male and female bodies. Some gods were understood to behave in fashions that would turn the stomach of a slaughterhouse master while others would make a barroom stripper blush. (The twin gods, Orisis and Isis were said to have fallen in love and had sexual intercourse while in their mother's womb. From that union, came the Egyptian god Horus, known among the Greeks as Apollo.)[25]

The practice of creating gods truly appears to go back to those near the fountainhead of the human species. I remember my youthful chuckle the first time I read Isaiah 44:14-19. There, Isaiah spoke of a man who cut a tree. The man took some wood and built a fire to warm himself. Then, he baked bread and roasted his meat. While warming himself, he slowly carved for himself a god from a piece of the same wood. In my mind, I envisioned him sitting on a block of the wood while he carved, pausing long enough to whittle a sliver with which to pick his teeth while he labored. Satisfied with his carving, the man bows before the image and worships it.

However, before he worshiped it, he had to mentally create powers which he projected into the idol. When one creates an idol, we must ask, "Which is the greater? The creator or the created?" Arrogance rules all who create gods to their own liking. The arrogance is akin to the arrogance of Adam and Eve who placed their judgment above God's judgment. Indeed, in doing so, they fashioned themselves into little gods that arrogantly said by their actions, "Our judgment is superior to yours." "We don't need our Creator to tell us how to live our lives. We will rely on our own judgment to determine what is best for us." In effect, by placing their judgment above God's, Adam and Eve made themselves into little gods. One of the most insidious and gravest forms of idolatry is the deified self!

The idolatry of the modern church is dual. It is evident in arrogant disobedience to God's written word, and it is evident by the church and its clergy in the common practice of creating **non**-Biblical images of God.

Disputing the nature of God as represented in His written word, the Bible, much of the modern church has worked to create a god to its own liking. The practice is not new among people who have claimed to worship the true God. While Moses was on Mt. Sinai receiving the Ten Commandments from Jehovah the God of creation and their deliverer, the people were in the valley fashioning a god in the form of a golden calf *in which they vested the powers of Jehovah* (cf. Exodus 32:1-6).

No, we have seen no golden calves in our places of worship (yet). We of the modern church are much too sophisticated to create a god that one could see or touch. If we fashioned a god that could be seen and touched, we could more easily accept the charge of idolatry.

Mr. Webster tells us that an idol is a "false god." It is an image fashioned by human beings. Is there truly any essential difference between a god fashioned by the hands and a god fashioned by the mind? The only real difference is in the fact that we can see and handle one, but we cannot see or handle the other.

In your wallet or purse, you probably carry a photograph of your spouse or someone else that you love. You could show it to me and say, "This is how my mate looks." You probably also carry a *mental* photograph of your spouse. Only you can "see" it in your mind. In a similar way, you carry a mental "picture" of your mate's personality. You could also choose to "show" me that mental picture of him or her. You might tell me if your mate is loving or unloving, kind or unkind, forgiving or grudge-carrying, optimistic or pessimistic, honest or dishonest, warm or cold, and you could tell me more. By the time you quit talking, you would have helped me to gain a rather clear image of the essence of your spouse. Your description might be so thorough that when we part, I would feel that I know him or her. I will carry that "image" away with me. I may not know how he or she looks, but I have an image of that personality in my mind.

When we create an image of God that varies from the image of God as revealed in the person of Jesus Christ, we hold a false image. We hold an idol of our own making.

Much of the modern church has disliked, disapproved, and abandoned God as revealed in Jesus, creating instead, an image of God to its own liking. Anything we see in God that we dislike, we try to change to our liking. Following the behavior of the Israelites at the foot of Mt. Sinai, the image is called God. Whatever the modern church or its individual members dislike about God, they create an image that suits its desires. The Biblical image of God as the Creator often has been abandoned and replaced by a mindless and Godless evolutionary process.

A God of love has been so overly emphasized that the God of judgment has been denied out of existence. In His stead, some have created a God only of love without the passion of anger. Many have even tried to deny that Jesus was angry when he upset the tables of the moneychangers in the temple and made a whip of cords and drove out the merchants. "He was not angry," we are likely to be told. "He was only righteously indignant."

The Biblical image of God bears both the face of love and of anger. Indeed, the anger may grow out of love. Any father becomes angry with those who harm his children! Even an earthly father is inclined to feel angry with his children who harm themselves. In effect, he says, "How dare you harm my child—even the one who lives in your skin." There is no character in him who never angers even in the face of some of the world's grave injustices.

My concordance lists thirty-seven references to God's anger. Large segments of the modern church seem to so much dread God's judgment, that they have created an image of an all-loving God who would never become angry or would never permit any person to suffer eternal destruction. The creation of such a mental image of God is nothing short of idolatry. Their mental creation is similar to the physical creation of the Israelites who fashioned the image of a golden calf and tried to endow it with the powers of Jehovah. We will worship the God of Heaven and Earth as the Bible reveals Him, or we will not truly worship Him at all.

For a short time in my early years, I was a part of the fellowship of a church in which the leadership openly denied the deity of Jesus the Christ. Those who came seeking the Christ heard that Jesus was only a good man of ancient history who taught the highest moral/ethical code ever spoken by man. They had created an image of God different from the God of the New Testament. But they called it God. Is it unfair to charge that church with idolatry?

Jesus was, indeed, a man in history. However, He is more. He is a person of pre-history and will yet live after the last word has been written by the last historian. Since God truly broke into history by taking on human flesh— by becoming incarnate—in the person of Jesus the Christ, we will better understand God by looking at Jesus.[26]

One of Jesus' closest and most faithful followers (disciples) said of Him, "In the beginning was the Word, and the Word was with God, and the word *was* God. . . . All things were made by him" (John 1:1-3). Any reading of the next 30 verses of John's account of the Gospel makes clear that John was speaking of Jesus of Nazareth.

Not only did John make such a claim, Jesus made an even stronger claim of himself. To the "woman at the well" Jesus announced that He was the Messiah (John 4:4-26). Even she knew of Isaiah's prophesy that the Messiah would be God in human flesh (God incarnate), "the Mighty God, the Everlasting Father" (Isaiah 9:6). Was Jesus deluded at the level of the old gentleman I once saw at the State Mental Hospital at Mandeville, Louisiana?

The fellow was so weak that to walk, he needed to be assisted by two aides. Yet he wanted us to know that he was the "Father of God."

Jesus left us with only three possible conclusions about His identity. He was a schizophrenic lunatic, a lying charlatan, or He was God in human flesh proclaiming truth when He told some astonished listeners, "Before Abraham was, I am." He was claiming divinity and his listeners knew it. They could not tolerate such blasphemy. They wanted to stone Him to death. (John 8:56-59) The Greek verb used for "I am" is a present tense verb of an infinite time-linear dimension. It says, "I always was, I now am, and I always shall be." Here, Jesus identified Himself as eternally co-existent with His Father, Jehovah. We get this name from the Hebrew name for God, YHWH. (The Hebrews wrote no vowels.) Since God's name was the most sacred of all sounds, for many centuries no one would speak His name for fear of "taking God's name in vain." Consequently, to this day no one is certain of the correct pronunciation.

Although linguistic scholars of the Hebrew language have struggled to understand the meaning of God's name, Jehovah, the generally accepted meaning may be stated as, "I am who I have always been and who I shall always be." Jesus identified Himself with this Eternal One. Any church that tolerates the projection of any other image of Jesus leads its people into idolatry.

Many unconsciously create a false image of God. In the late 1950s, I served three years in a program of Internship and Residency for Hospital Chaplains which included training for counseling. My responsibilities required that I spend fifty percent of my time among my hospitalized patients and fifty percent with Nursing Students and hospital employees.

On one occasion, a counselee was talking about her father when I realized she had changed the subject and was talking about God. The transition had been too subtle for me to notice immediately. When I cautiously inquired, I found that she used the same adjectives to describe the personalities of both God and her father. She later recognized that she had taken her perception of the personality of her father (his image) and had superimposed that image onto God. For her, the personalities of her father and God were identical. Her image of the personality of her father stood as a barrier to the image of the personality of God as seen in Jesus. Over the next several years, I counseled with others who seemed to have done the same thing.

When I began to counsel with women who had been sexually abused by their fathers, almost invariably, I found a cautious distance between those women and God. One fifty-seven year old lady said, "When I hear you say that God loves me, I have a hard time trying not to remember Daddy raping me and saying, "I love you—I love you — I love you"—all the time he was doing it to me. . . . Even after all these years, every time I hear the word God, I see Daddy's face."

Another was a thirty-seven year old woman whose father had warned her and her three sisters that if they ever did anything "bad wrong" he would take them under the house, hang them by their hair, and cut off their heads. He never defined, "Bad wrong." After that, each time he screamed at them, they wondered if they had done something "bad wrong." "My fear of my father is interfering with my relationship with God. The adult in me knows the difference. But there is a child back in there somewhere who can't seem to tell the difference between my daddy and God. Every one of us girls has lived in fear of my daddy and every one of us has been scared to death of God."

After hearing numerous stories similar to those two, I began to wonder if these reactions to childhood experiences were only rare isolated coincidences, or if they were common occurrences. I had read somewhere that we human beings tend to look at our fathers and assume that God is "just like my daddy." But those seemed to be opinions without supporting social scientific research.

I had been startled on one occasion when I overheard Lisa, my small daughter, engaged in conversation about God while sitting in my sister-in-law's lap. "Where do you think God is," my sister-in-law asked. Lisa responded, "I don't know, but sometimes I feel Him real close — so close I can almost feel His whiskers — just like my daddy's." The more I listened at the bedside of my patients and to my counselees behind the closed doors of my office, the more interested I was becoming.

My curiosity could be satisfied only by research. I entered a doctoral program on the condition that I would be taught how to research my interest. I found that little effort had been made to study the correlation between people's perception of the personality of their parents and their perception of the personality of God. And reports of the little research that had been accomplished had been published only in psychological journals that the general public nor ministers would rarely read. I found that in the U.S. only one small prior research project had been conducted in some New England states. Two others had been conducted in Europe. My project numbered more respondents than all others combined up to that time.

Although each of the few studies used completely dissimilar research instruments, all four projects came to the same conclusion. In four different parts of the world, we independently found a significant correlation between the perceptions of the personalities of fathers and perceptions of the personality of God. The strength of the correlations between the perceptions of the personality of mothers and the personality of God were significant but somewhat weaker than correlations between fathers and God.

I know of at least twenty additional research projects that have replicated my study, using my research instrument. Evidence mounts that leads us to conclude that we human beings are born with the propensity to look at our father and conclude that God is "just like my daddy."[27] The studies further suggest that the personalities of the parents may be more consequential in the development of a concept of the personality of God than formal religious education.[28]

On first glance, some may think that these studies support Sigmund Freud's declaration that there is no God — that man merely projects onto the cosmos a god of his own making that fits the image of his own father. I have dismissed Freud's opinion after drawing conclusions based on the social scientific evidence reviewed in my dissertation. Too much space would be required to debate it here. I will simply quote Edward Stein and move on.

"It is perfectly possible that the way in which the Ground of Being made himself known, revealed himself, was by making man biologically dependent upon human parents and prone to such projection. Psychological explanation does not account for ontological reality, however much it may throw light onto it."[29]

However psychologically influenced our image of God may be, it is the responsibility of the church to uphold the Biblical image of God and none other. Any image of God that does not reflect the image of God as revealed in the person of Jesus is a false image and therefore, an idolatrous image. History reveals no point in which humankind has not been a creator of images that have been called gods. "Uncivilized man," with his hands, created images of gold, or stone or wood and worshiped them as gods. "Civilized man" with his mind has created images with his mind and worshiped them as God.

Anything that the modern church has seen, but has not liked, has been tailored to suit the church. Much of the church has denied Jesus' virgin birth. Others deny the His deity. Others deny Jesus' sacrificial atonement by His crucifixion. (Within the past week, someone told me that reference to the "blood of Christ" is forbidden from the pulpit in his church.) Many deny Christ's resurrection from the dead.

How do the "scholars" who are permitted to dictate "truth" to the church arrive at their conclusions? The God of the Bible has been under attack since the dawn of Rationalism and the Age of Enlightenment in the seventeenth and eighteenth century. This system of thought holds that the human mind is supreme. Those who buy into the rationalistic philosophy rely on "natural light." When applied to theology or ethics, this "natural light" replaces supernatural revelation with reason.

This system asserts that the miracles of Jesus "don't make sense" because they do not fit into the normal laws of physics within the universe. Therefore,

Jesus did not perform miracles. I recently read after one "scholar," that Jesus performed no miracle when he fed more than five thousand people with five loafs of bread and two fishes (Matthew 14:13-21). He declared that while Jesus fed the people, he stood in front of a cave in which he previously had stashed large amounts of bread and fish. His disciples secretly handed Him the food and the thousands believed he was performing a miracle.

Some "scholars" also have concluded that since the Virgin Birth is illogical by defying "laws of nature," it is only a myth fabricated by the Gospel writers.

The "scholars" tell us that Jesus did not really die on the cross. While still on the cross, He became comatose or someone drugged him to feign death. He later revived and his disciples believed he had resurrected from the dead.

They also tell us that since everyone knows that a dead person cannot rise from the dead, the Gospel writers lied by writing that Jesus resurrected from the dead. (A Gallup survey concluded that twenty-five percent of Americans do not know why Christians celebrate Easter.)

Resurrection from the dead is not rational. Within the past week a renowned (Christian?) writer came to my city for the purpose of disclaiming Jesus' resurrection from the dead. He calls himself a "New Testament scholar" with access to the "ancient Greek texts." Of course he has. The most ancient and most reliable texts are available for study by him and many hundreds of scholars who fully accept the reality of the resurrection as described in the New Testament. He has access to no texts and archeological discoveries that have not been open for study by thousands of scholars for many years. However, he gained headlines in the local newspaper. The unusual — the bazaar always gains media attention. If someone came to town to lecture at the local university on the marvelous miracle of Jesus' resurrection, he would not have received a moment of media attention.

When "scholars" begin with the premise that the Bible is inaccurate, they can, and do, create any version of "reality"—any version of "truth" that their minds can fabricate. And since they are the "scholars," who of the general public could possibly argue against their conclusions? These pseudo-intellectuals do not stop by denying Jesus' resurrection.

Since the ascension defies gravity and possibly recognizes at least some degree of divinity, the "natural light" of reason tells us that Jesus could not possibly have ascended into the heavens as described by the New Testament (Acts 1:6-11). (One "scholar" has declared that Jesus simply walked up the side of a mountain and out of sight into a hovering cloud. He later slipped away and lived in a remote village among the Essenes until he died several years later.) And such tales are accepted, not only by the general public, but by large segments of the church by the leadership of the pastor!

Who can argue with "scholars?" (I have earned a Masters degree and two doctoral degrees and was honored with a third doctorate after I conducted several post-doctoral research projects. I earned the rank of "Scholar" in the Society of Scholars of Oxford Graduate School and served as the society's Chairman of the Board of Governors for sixteen years. I promote scholarship and respect true scholars.)

How do the "scholars" who work to create and sell their non-Biblical image of God arrive at conclusions before traveling their university lecture circuits, writing their books, and even translating their version of the Gospels? Let's look at one of the most publicized groups of recent years.

A group of "scholars" that numbered from time to time between forty and seventy-four devised an "ingenious" method of arriving at "truth." They have gained renown for their "scholarly" work reported in their many writings. This group met under the title of "the Jesus Seminar." They gathered from time to time over a six-year period to determine which passages within the Gospels were authentic and which passages were fictional. Obviously, before they met, they had already concluded that much within the four Gospels of the New Testament were not authentic. When they met, they made their decisions by *voting* with one of four colored beads.

After reading each verse of the Gospels, each "scholar" dropped a red bead into a container when the "scholar" voted his belief that the passage was completely accurate. They often voted on their belief in the accuracy of an individual word or phrase within a verse. As the container was passed around the room, the "scholar" dropped in a pink bead if he or she believed the passage read somewhat close to what Jesus actually said. They dropped a gray bead if they believed Jesus did not say the words, but they held traces of something He possibly said, and they dropped a black bead into the container if the "scholar" was certain that the words attributed to Jesus did not come close to what He said. By this method these "enlightened scholars" tell us what Jesus "really" said and did. Based on their decisions made by the casting of beads, the participants have written their books and their translation of the Gospels.

These "scholars" seem to pity us poor ignorant souls who continue to believe that Jesus really taught His disciples "the Lord's Prayer" and believe that Jesus told Nicodemus he needed to be "born again" (from above). Furthermore, they want you to know that John 3:16 simply does not "sound like anything Jesus would have said." Lazy thinkers tend to conclude, "If it is written in a book by as scholar, it must be true." That which is novel gets media attention.

A few years ago, more than half a million teen-agers convened in one of our major cities to enhance their Christian growth. My local newspaper gave it less than two inches of print in the back pages. Who's interested in reading of teen-agers going about their business and doing something that may help themselves and others? That's not news! However, in the same newspaper, two teen-aged boys got nearly a quarter of a page of attention because they had stolen a car, robbed a convenience store, and shot the owner. That's unusual. That's news! The unusual gets attention.

What competent scholar gets media coverage by saying that the Bible is true and accurate as it is written? That's not newsworthy. Those who create a new gospel (without good news) with a new image of its God, get the media attention. And thousands both outside the church and inside the church blindly accept that which is promoted by the "scholars."

Recognizing that no theory of biblical criticism has ever stood for more than one generation, I long ago lost patience with their proponents. I found a good reason to do so.

I once found an anonymously written pamphlet that I thought worthy of distributing among my patients throughout the hospital in which I served as chaplain. I showed it to an associate, Charles (Charlie) W. Burrows, and we agreed that it was excellent, but we each thought of additions we would like to insert. He inserted his and I inserted mine. The insertions blended so well with the pre-existing pamphlet that six months later, neither Charlie nor I could remember what part was original, what was his, and what was mine. If we could not differentiate our separate writings from that of another writer after only six months, I seriously question the ability of "scholars" to determine what Jesus or Paul or Isaiah "really" did or did not do or say thousands of years after the fact.

However, since most people are not aware of the world of "biblical scholarship," if forty or more "scholars" say something, it must be true. In the words of The Rev. Dr. Charles Revis, a pastor in Bakersfield, California, "The solid body of material that disputes the conclusions of the Jesus Seminar seldom reached the everyday person."

For every scholar who denies the New Testament as it stands, thousands of others affirm its validity. The Jesus Seminar or others of their breed begin with the premise that the New Testament is in error, and they propose to "correct" it. However, with access to no sources that orthodox scholars do not have, one must suspect a high degree of arrogance that results in a false image of the Christ. Such a false image is nothing short of idolatry.

This writer finds it interesting that the "scholars" of the sort contributing to the Jesus Seminar have joined ranks with the most uninformed, uneducated men and women of our society. We live with the popular belief that the higher the level of one's education, the less likely the person to believe the Bible to be the divinely inspired word of God. George Gallup's organization has found this to be *untrue*.

Dr Hollis Green has reported that when the editors of an internationally circulated humanist magazine read Gallup's report, they doubted the accuracy of that study. They conducted their own study. They were surprised to learn that only 45 percent of persons with only a high school education believe the Bible to be the inspired word of God. However, 64 percent of those with a college degree believed in the Bible's accuracy.

Mark Twain has been credited with having said that a lie can travel half way around the world while the truth is still putting its boots on. And someone else has said that "it is almost impossible to overtake, and kill, and bury a lie. If you do, someone will erect a monument over the grave, and the lie will be born again as an epitaph." Our "scholars" have persuaded many of Christ's church to deny Jesus' resurrection.

Others deny His ascension. If He did not ascend into Heaven, His dust remains somewhere in Palestine. A dead god cannot save from anything or to anything. A Messiah/Christ whose body rotted in some unidentified tomb has no Eternal Heavenly Kingdom. What say the Scriptures?

"Now if Christ be preached that he rose from the dead, how say some among you that there is no resurrection of the dead? But if there be no resurrection of the dead, then is Christ not risen: And if Christ be not risen, then is our preaching vain, and your faith is also vain. Yea, and we are found false witnesses of God; because we have testified of God that he raised up Christ: whom he raised not up, if so be that the dead rise not. For if the dead rise not, then is not Christ raised: And if Christ be not raised, your faith is vain; ye are yet in your sins"
(1 Corinthians 15:12-19).

But He lives! He lives!

CONCLUSION

Come now, and let us reason together,
 saith the Lord: though your sins be
as scarlet, they shall be as white as snow;
though they be red like crimson, they
shall be as wool. (Isa. 1:18)

When friends have learned that I was writing a book on seven deadly sins of dying churches, repeatedly, they have smiled and asked, "Only seven?" Indeed, perhaps you can name more, but in final analysis, we must recognize that Jesus reduced all sin to the violation of two commandments. He spoke them clearly. *"Thou shalt love the Lord thy God with all thy heart, and with all thy soul, and with all thy mind. This is the first and great commandment. And the second is like unto it, Thou shalt love thy neighbor as thyself"* (Matt. 22:37-39).

Every page of this book has called attention to the habitual practice of sin among the membership of a major population of Christ's church. I would not waste my time or yours by calling attention to a problem without offering a solution. Life has taught me that any fool can take a hammer and destroy a good piece of furniture, but only a skilled craftsman can build one.[30]

Across the ages, God has provided a process by which his people can deal constructively with their sin.

Both John the Baptist and Jesus began early in their ministry to demand repentance (cf. Matt. 3:2; Matt. 4:17). They did not always make the demand with un-offensive language. John the Baptist lost his head after calling Herod Antipas an adulterer, and Jesus was crucified after calling the religious leaders of His day a bunch of hypocrites, whitewashed tombs, vipers, and other unflattering names. Despite the anticipated consequences, both John the Baptist and Jesus called for repentance. But we do not repent until we admit that we are wrong—that we are going in the wrong direction.

However, some people are so self-directed that they refuse to follow the instructions of the best authority. A man I knew in years gone by serves as a perfect illustration. He and his wife were driving from out of North Carolina to Knoxville, Tennessee. At a fork in the highway, he turned left. His wife spoke up and told him that he had made a wrong turn. They were going toward Sylva, NC instead of Knoxville, TN. I'm not sure his wife ever let him live down his response. "I saw the sign saying Knoxville is to the right, but I've got a feeling that the sign is wrong." He was forced to confess his error when they arrived in Sylva. Only after he admitted his error did he turn around to go back toward Knoxville. If we put that in theological language, we can say that he had to admit (confess) his error before he could repent (turn and go in the right direction).

That part of the church and that part of its leadership that has been practicing sin must first admit error before it can repent. (However, arrogant pride is difficult to overcome.)

Unfortunately, we are looking at a matter as old as Adam and Eve in the Garden of Eden. Adam and Eve were guilty of the sin of pride. This kind of pride carries the attitude that says, "I know best. I don't need God, or the Bible, or anyone else to give me instruction." Such pride does not place oneself on a par with God. Such an attitude places one's judgment *above* God's. "I will obey my own instructions." Sylva, NC is a pleasant little town. My friend's arrival there was no great penalty—only a couple of gallons of gasoline and an hour of time. He could turn and go in the right direction. However, they who continue to err until they arrive at their unexpected and undesired destination will find repentance no longer an option. My even greater concern is for the large number of people they harm by their influence while they travel en route to their destination.

We can rejoice in the Gospel.[31] Whatever the sin, those who confront their sin, and repent by surrendering to the Lordship of the Messiah—the Christ—the King, will find Him waiting with open arms, waiting to forgive, waiting to begin a redemptive, re-creative work, waiting to lead the enjoyable trip Home. He is still calling, "Come. Keep on following Me henceforth and forever more." We rejoice in knowing that we live under the God of another chance.

INDEX

ENDNOTES

1   Based on things I read, I fear that churches in the United Kingdom may be in even more danger than churches in the United States. I strongly recommend M. Phillips' book, *Londonistan,* (New York: Encounter Books, 2006). It has great implications for every person on North American soil. I have made it required reading for all of my candidates for Master's and Doctor of Philosophy degrees.

2   Hollis L. Green, *Why Churches Die,* (Minneapolis, MN: Bethany Fellowship Inc., 1971), p. 31.

3   *Ibid,* p. 29.

4   *Ibid,* p. 54f.

5   *Ibid, p. 16 & 36.*

6   The Biblical use of the word "redeemer" refers to "one who sets free."

7   *De Defect. Orac.* § 17.

8   David Smith, *The Days of His Flesh,* (New York: Harper & Brothers, nd) p. 7.

9   Ann Wroe, *Pontius Pilate,* (New York: Random House, 1999), p. 137.

10   For the purpose of making administrative reports I kept records. During the thirty-onee years that I served at the bedside of my patients, I engaged in approximately 300,000 "behind closed doors" conversations.

11   The word "righteous" was borrowed from the carpenter's craft. It refers to that which is absolutely upright or plumb. That which is "unrighteous" is not plumb. A builder must plumb a wall. It cannot plumb itself.

12   The New Testament recognizes two separate kinds of "life." When speaking of physical life, it uses a form of the word "*bios.*" When speaking of spiritual life, it uses a form of the word, "*zoe.*"

13 Wm. G. Justice, *God in the Hands of Angry Sinners* (Bloomington, IN: Authorhouse 2004).

14 Wm. G. Justice, *The Nature of God as Revealed in Jesus* (New York: iUniverse) 2005. I needed this entire book to adequately deal with this issue.

15 Before I retired, I was dually licensed by the state of Tennessee as a Marriage and Family Therapist and as a Professional Counselor. I was also a clinical member of the American Association For Marriage and Family Therapy with more than 20,000 hours of counseling experience.

16 The word "charity" is another word for love and is so translated repeatedly in 1 Corinthians 13 in the King James Version of the Bible. This chapter in the New Testament is one of the best descriptions of love's behavior ever written.

17 Karl Menninger, *Whatever Became of Sin* (New York: Hawthorn Books, Inc., 1973).

18 That which Jesus spoke here seems appropriate to all the Law.

19 Green, *Why Christianity Fails in America* (Crystal Springs TN: GlobalEdAdcance Press 2007), p. 38.

20 *Ibid* p. 142f.

21 A teen-age girl who had been a member of a church, attending Sunday School and worship services since childhood expressed surprise when I informed her that indiscriminant sex with various boy-friends was sinful, immoral, and harmful to her personality.

22 John MacArthur, *The Gospel According to Jesus* (Grand Rapids, Academic Books, Zondervan Publishing House), 1988, p.59.

23 J. Gerald Harris, The Christian Index, "What's the Value of Adding Zeros?", Vol. 182, No. 21, October 23, 2003.

24 As I write, beside me is a catalogue from Sadigh Gallery Ancient Art, Inc., 303 Fifth Avenue, Suite 1603, New York, NY, 10016. Among hundreds of archeological items, they list for sale probably more than a hundred idols that range from two thousand to four thousand years old.

25 Wm. G. Justice, *Gifts for the gods: Pagan and Christian Sacrifices*, (Lincoln, NE: iUniverse, 2009).

26 *The Nature of God as Revealed in Jesus* (New York: iUniverse, 2005).

27   These studies point to the urgency for fathers to live "godly" lives. I know of no research among persons who have been reared without a father-image within the home. What are the implications for children for who are shifted among twenty or more foster homes? Many questions are yet to be studied for answer. These materials were taken from a dissertation by William G. Justice, *A Comparative Study of the Language People Use To Describe the Personalities of God and Their Earthly Parents* submitted in partial fulfillment of the requirements for the degree of Doctor of Philosophy for Oxford Graduate School, Crystal Springs (Dayton) TN. Copies of the dissertation, LD000963 are available from Universities Microfilm International, 300 N. Zeeb Rd. Ann Arbor, MI, 48106.

28   We need additional research that would examine the development of perceptions of God in homes that have no father figure living on the scene.

29   Edward Stein, *Guilt: Theory and Therapy*, (Philadelphia: Westminister Press, 1968), p. 193.

30   When I pause from writing today, I will go to my woodworking shop to finish building an armoire for our bedroom.

31   In the days of Jesus' flesh, the Greek word that is translated for us as "good news," "gospel," or "glad tidings" was usually associated with a report of political importance. It was not used to speak of just any welcomed report. It carried the idea of good news of public importance, worthy of being carried by a runner, and worthy of holding a celebration when received.

About the Author

Wm. G. Justice, DMin, DPhil, DLitt, has authored 15 previous books and over 200 articles in his field. He has been a student of history throughout his adult years. He has taught the Bible for 54 years, having begun while Piloting B-29 bombers during the Korean War. While serving 31 years as a professional bedside hospital chaplain, he earned licenses as a Professional Counselor and as a Marriage and Family Therapist and taught off-campus courses to candidates for bachelors, masters, and doctoral degrees for twelve different colleges, seminaries, and graduate schools. Although retired from hospital ministry and counseling, he continues to teach courses in Marriage Relations and A History of the Integration of Religion and Society as a Distinguished Professor of Religion and Society at Oxford Graduate School.

Printed in the United States
by Baker & Taylor Publisher Services